MEISSEN
PORTRAIT FIGURES

MEISSEN
PORTRAIT FIGURES

LEN AND YVONNE ADAMS

MAGNA BOOKS

This edition published 1992
by Magna Books, Magna road, Wigston,
Leicester, LE8 2ZH
produced by the
Promotional Reprint Company Limited.

Printed in China

ISBN 1 85422 318 6

Contents

Acknowledgements

We have always held the view that in the world of antiques those people with a love of porcelain are the most sympathetic, and since starting this book the help and encouragement we have received has more than endorsed this belief.

We wish to thank our many friends amongst collectors, dealers and the auction houses for their help and for lending photographs to fill the gaps in our own albums. Some wish to remain anonymous, but include the following:

Messrs Christies, Mr Geoffrey Godden; Mr and Mrs H. R. Hart; Mrs Margot Newman; Mr Michael Newman; Mr Albert Potts; Prof. Dr J. Rafael; Mr Henry Sandon; Messrs Sothebys; Mr Robert Williams.

List of colour plates

Introduction

For hundreds of years men have been fascinated by the delicacy of porcelain. Marco Polo's book *Il Milione* was the source of many legends about porcelain in Europe and gave rise to the belief that it had magic qualities. It was said to be able to ward off illness and to be a protection against poison (as usual with old sayings and myths, there is probably some truth in this, as porcelain can be kept cleaner than wood or pewter). The high esteem in which the early pieces were held can be seen in fifteenth- and sixteenth-century paintings where people are shown holding precious blue and white porcelain vessels as if proclaiming to the world their wealth and standing. Marco Polo gave it the name 'Porcellana' from the small Mediterranean cowrie shell which to him resembled Chinese porcelain.

It was not until the discovery of the sea passage to India that the transport of porcelain from the Far East made it possible for the wealthy of Europe to collect anything like the amount they craved. However, even though porcelain became slightly more available, it was still formidably expensive.

Augustus II, Elector of Saxony and King of Poland (known as 'Augustus the Strong' not for his leadership nor his not inconsiderable strength, but for his having fathered more than 350 children), was an ardent collector of porcelain, which he referred to as his 'malady'; so much so, that in 1717 he exchanged 600 soldiers from his army for 127 pieces of Chinese porcelain owned by King Frederick William of Prussia. Augustus was not content with his already immense collection, but dreamed of having almost everything in his castle made of porcelain.

It was not surprising, therefore, that he took a great interest in the experiments made by Ehrenfried Walther von Tschirnhaus, a nobleman and optics scientist who had already established several glass works. Von Tschirnhaus was a mathemetician and physicist, having studied at the University of Leyden. He made several visits to France to study their scientific innovations in the hope of improving such things in Saxony, and also visited Holland, where he learned how to make a kiln. His most important constructions were gigantic concave mirrors and burning glasses designed to obtain the utmost concentration of solar heat. He was able to fuse some minerals, i.e. quartz and chalk, but at this stage was convinced that porcelain was a fusion of a glasslike composition. However, despite these experiments by von Tschirnhaus, who believed that it was essential to discover the secret of hard-paste porcelain in order to stop the enormous flow of gold and silver out of Saxony to pay for Chinese porcelain, Augustus II still really believed that porcelain was produced by alchemy; as it was still believed that gold could be made from the philosopher's stone. Therefore when the young apothocary's apprentice Johann Friedrich Böttger appeared in Dresden in 1705, fleeing from King Frederick of Prussia because he had failed to fulfil his boast of being able to turn base metal into gold, he was seized by Augustus' troops, incarcerated in the Fortress of Königstein, and told to continue his work. When von Tschirnhaus heard of the young apothocary, he gave him the task of trying to find out how to make porcelain. He was given access to the kilns designed by von Tschirnhaus, instructed in the use of mathematical equations, and supplied with scientific literature.

Thus, in collaboration in 1707 Böttger and von Tschirnhaus were able to produce a brownish-red stoneware similar to that made by the Chinese. On 15 January 1708, they produced a small white bowl. Sadly, ten months later von Tschirnhaus died, but Böttger continued with the work, and was able to report to the King in March 1709 that he was producing good white porcelain with a fine white glaze 'equal to that from the East Indies'.

The two essential ingredients were the infusible clay known as kaolin and the fusible, a feldspar known as petuntse. Feldspar melts to form a natural cemment that holds together the infusible clay. This porcelain body was then covered with a glaze made of the same feldspar, mixed with potash. The glaze would unite perfectly with the body. The original was first fired to a 'biscuit' state and then, after glazing, fired to a temperature of around 1350° centigrade.

Thus the Meissen Porcelain Manufactury was started in 1712 with twenty-three men, all working prisoners who were not artists, but very good craftsmen; and this was the beginnings of the greatest ceramic enterprise Europe has ever known.

In the early days, only faithful copies of Chinese ware were made, but the King also wanted his beloved porcelain to be made in the European style. In 1729 he ordered his palace to be doubled in size and to have a chapel with fittings of porcelain, including a pulpit, organ and pipes. Böttger, who had been a virtual prisoner, had turned to drink and died at the age of 37 in 1719. From quite early on, modellers such as Georg Fritzsche and Johann Gottlieb Kirchner were employed. Both Fritzsche and Kirchner produced some very exciting pieces, particularly the latter; however, they were not able to work at the speed demanded by the King, and Kirchner was said to drink very heavily and was accused of laziness. So a young stone carver by the name of Johann Joachim Kaendler, aged 25, was employed as another modeller in 1731. The son of a Protestant pastor, he had been apprenticed to a stone-mason sculptor named Benjamin Thomae. It was from this date that the wonderful European porcelain figures—to be so widely collected and copied—were made. It was under Kaendler's influence that religious and mythological figures were made as porcelain interpretations of statues in the royal parks and palaces, and he started a trend which was to continue throughout the history of the Meissen factory – that of taking inspiration from engravings and paintings, particularly from the very extensive royal collection.

Kaendler's artistic sense and appreciation of current fashion was truly amazing, as was his ability to interpret the strong baroque style and later the gaiety of the rococo in such phenomenal numbers. He produced thousands of models in his forty-three years at Meissen, and in his very first week made three birds larger than life. These large birds and animals, made for the palace, were of great importance to the King, and although the enormous firing cracks show the difficulty in firing such large pieces at that time, they do illustrate Kaendler's extraordinary skill and determination at an early age.

In 1733 Kaendler was made Model Master, which gave him some of the administration of the factory as well as control of all the modelling. The organization of the factory was made up of the Director or representative of the King, namely Count Brühl; the Model Master and the assistant modellers; the Arcanist, who was responsible for the preparation of the raw materials; the kiln master, who was responsible for the glazing; the moulder, who made moulds from the cut up section of clay or wood figures previously made by the modellers; the repairer, who assembled the moulded porcelain parts with the help of clay mixed with water, known as 'slip'; the painters, who worked in enamels, and lastly the gilders.

In 1735 Kaendler was joined by an assistant modeller, Johann Frederick Eberlein, in 1739 by Johann Gottlieb Ehder, in 1743 by Peter Reinicke, and in 1748 by Frederich Elias Meyer. Unfortunately in 1749 Eberlein died of tuberculosis; he was followed in October 1750 by Ehder, who leaped from the castle wall to avoid the night-watch after staying too long at an inn, and died of his injuries soon afterwards. These men were greatly missed by Kaendler, who apparently was never jealous of his assistants, but encouraged them to do their own work as well as assist him, as can be seen in many individual creations such as Peter Reinicke's Cries of Paris series and Italian Comedy series for the Duke of Weissenfels. Apart from making many of his own fine models, including a large village for Count Brühl's table, Ehder is known to have made a set of false teeth with clay gums! Unfortunately we do not know who the lucky recipient was. There have been stories over the years that Kaendler disliked Meyer's way of making small heads on his figures, or even that Kaendler caused this to happen during the firing in the kiln, which caused shrinkage. This seems highly unlikely, and it would appear far more possible that this was Meyer's way of expressing the asymmetrical rococo spirit and elegance.

The influence of Augustus the Strong's personal taste remained even after his death in 1733. His son Augustus III did not have quite the same passion for porcelain as his father, but he did realize the potential prestige and commercial value of the factory. He gave overall control to his Chief Minister, Count Heinrich von Brühl, a wealthy and influential man who was a great connoisseur of all forms of art, particularly the magnificent baroque; and it was he, as well as the King, who supplied the factory with many drawings and engravings for inspiration.

The variety of things made in porcelain was quite remarkable. There were not only the massive table services and figures and groups, which were made originally as table decorations, but according to a 1739 stock list there were held in a warehouse such things as key-rings, swinging-kettles, chamber pots, clock cases, temples, writing stands, bells, holy water pots, beads for rosaries, shoe buckles, syphons, and water pails. On 4 February 1745 Sir Charles Hanbury-Williams, the English Ambassador to the Polish Court, wrote home to his relative Henry Fox: 'I believe I never told you that the King of Poland (Augustus III) has given me a set of china for a table of thirty covers, which would have cost here Fifteen Hundred Pounds . . . I design to send a description of the dessert service to Lady Caroline (Fox). He did this, and also included descriptions of 166 figures that were part of the table decorations, of which 54 were of a pastoral nature and 34 of hunting. He also later wrote home recounting his participation at a dinner party given by Count Brühl for two hundred people, where he was amazed at a porcelain fountain at least 8 feet high which was set in the centre of the table when dessert was served, and which ran with rose water and was said to have cost £6000. Horace Walpole also wrote: 'Jellies, biscuits, sugar plums and creams have long given way to Harlequins, Gondoliers, Turks, Chinese and Shepherdesses of Saxon China.'

This ability to create masterpieces in such a difficult medium as clay was the envy of all the other European porcelain factories. Such was the influence that Meissen exerted over the other factories that whether through laziness on their part, or true admiration, an enormous number of figures were copied by Chelsea, Bow, Derby, etc., often in soft paste. At the beginning Meissen had tried to keep the recipe for making hard paste porcelain a secret, but by the late 1740s so many of their workmen had defected that porcelain factories began to open all over Europe. But by this stage Meissen's technique was so far advanced, and the modelling of Kaendler and his assistants so sophisticated, that it was not until the end of the eighteenth century that they proved any threat. Production was also so vast that in 1756, at the onset of the Seven Years' War, when Prussian troops broke into the home of Count Brühl they found over three thousand porcelain figures and groups.

It is important to remember that no Meissen model is unique or one of a kind. Although rare after some 250 years, and always costly, several of each model were always made. In fact, of the 34 animals and 27 birds Kaendler created in 1734 on court orders, 16 were made of each; probably in the fear that some might not survive the firing in the kiln, or that the King would want to give some away; and several of each have survived to this day. The figures were made to be cut into sections, moulds taken of the sections, and these pieces fitted together by the repairers. Because of this process, variations occur. Therefore, no one can say one particular piece is the original. All that can be said is that a figure has the artistic flow, correct colour combinations and colour of paste for that particular period. Just because an arm is at a different angle to that of a famous piece in a museum does not make it of a different date. However, what must be guarded against are the pieces that were originally made in white only, and then decorated at some later date in a London or Paris workshop. The great dealer/politician Schimmelman bought and sold warehouses of Meissen porcelain – coloured, white, and even unfinished – with the approval of King Frederick of Prussia after the Seven Years' War, apparently for services rendered to the Prussian army. The continuous and varied ownerships of the porcelain, and the confusion of war, were probably the means by which so much porcelain made its way to the studios of independent decorators, particularly in Paris, where they proliferated both before and after the French Revolution.

Although not all pieces bear a factory mark, the famous Crossed Swords mark originated in the second half of the 1720s and at the beginning was sometimes incorporated with such marks as M.P.M. or K.P.M. However, on the unglazed bases of figures the mark frequently disappeared during firing, and so it was decided to put the mark on the back of the figures. But even this is not an infallible way of identifying these early figures, as the marks were put on by apprentices who did not always perform their duties properly, and also gave great variations to the shape and size of the Crossed Swords. It must be remembered that they were not thinking of the next two hundred years of collectors. Indeed, it is surprising that they marked their porcelain at all, as they quite rightly considered themselves pre-eminent in European porcelain and were sure that no discerning eye could mistake a copy for the original Meissen. The Turkish market was large and important to the Meissen factory, but the Crossed Swords mark was not generally welcomed. The Turkish importer in 1730 refused to accept Meissen porcelain with this mark, as in the Moslem world it was mistaken for the Christian cross. Many figures and groups bear impressed numbers, but although over the years various attempts have been made to relate these numbers to the years when the figures were made, it is more likely these numbers were merely a convenient way of keeping track of the models, as recent research by the Meissen archivists has shown that some of Kaendler's records do not tie up with the numbers on his models, and in any case some of the records were destroyed during the Seven Years' War.

The Meissen factory had achieved very sophisticated heights early in its history, and in 1740 had main dealers in Amsterdam, Augsberg, Berlin, Breslau, Belgrade, Brunswick, Frankfurt, Geneva, Hamburg, Hanover, London, Magdeburg, Marienberg, Macedonia, Paris, St Petersburg, Vienna and Warsaw.

Augustus II had promised great prosperity to the town of Meissen when he started the porcelain factory, and by 1751 the workers and their families had increased the population by more than 1800. This did indeed create a great deal of prosperity for the town, but many records and town laws have revealed that the factory workers were treated badly and despised by the townspeople, and attempts were made to charge them exorbitant prices for food, rents and even funerals, and that petty offences brought down on them very heavy fines which caused bitterness on both sides, even down to the factory workers boycotting the locally brewed beer. This state of affairs was not finally settled until 1754, when the local inhabitants were made to realize just how much money the factory brought to their town.

In 1756 the Seven Years' War started between Prussia and a European alliance of Austria, Saxony, France and Russia. Russia, with no experience of continental European affairs, but with an army of 80,000 men, crossed the Prussian border and defeated Frederick's forces. However, the Russian Court was divided in its loyalties. The Empress Elizabeth was on the side of the Austrians etc., but her son and heir favoured the Prussians. Once again the Russian forces defeated the Prussian army in 1759, and a successful raid on Berlin almost spelt doom for Frederick's military survival. In January 1762, however, the Empress

Elizabeth died, and Peter III ascended the throne. With Peter's sympathies towards Prussia, their war with Frederick was ended. This was considered to be a token of divine providence by Frederick, for if the Empress Elizabeth had not died, who can say what the outcome of the war, and consequently the future of the Meissen factory would have been. Having failed to make any efforts to secure itself militarily, Saxony was easily over-run by Prussian troops very early on in the war, and Meissen passed into the hands of Frederick the Great of Prussia.

Although Frederick was also a great lover of porcelain, his way of showing this was to raid the warehouses and take the porcelain back to Prussia; he also tried to persuade the Meissen workmen to work for him at his Berlin factory. Most of the kilns were destroyed during the war, and many of the staff scattered, but although a small amount of work was carried out during the first few years of the war, the blows suffered by the factory at the end and after the war greatly impaired their lead in porcelain manufacture in Europe. This was further injured by other factories opening up across Europe at this time, frequently with former Meissen workers, and more importantly, by the expansion and artistic lead now taken by the royal factory at Sèvres.

Kaendler's ability to interpret the baroque and rococo did not, in old age, encompass the fashion of the late eighteenth century, the Neoclassical revival. The vitality and truthfulness of the modelling were no longer appreciated. Sentimentality and artificial prettiness now ruled, and other modellers such as the Frenchman Acier were employed. Kaendler's inability to work in this new style is patently obvious, and thus this particular era came to an end. Although the factory has continued to this day, it has never again had the pre-eminence over all other porcelain factories that it enjoyed in the eighteenth century.

Having been captured by the allure of these wonderful Meissen figures and groups, after one or two purchases of different types a collector's taste will frequently change. When this happens, we try to steer them into collecting a particular series, as the search for the one piece that will fit in is a large part of the fun, and should the collection be sold at any time, a complete series with continuity is more valuable than a collection of diverse subjects. This is why the book has been organized on the basis of what we consider to be collectable series.

Over the last two hundred years fashions have of course changed. In the middle of the eighteenth century the standard classical education received by the middle and upper classes of Europe caused them to regard mythological subjects with great favour. Nowadays these are not so widely collected, which is a pity as they are wonderful pieces of sculpture. In the twentieth century the Italian Comedy series have been extremely popular, with much higher prices paid in comparison to other figures, but these prices too can fluctuate according to how many ardent collectors are chasing the same piece.

If investment, as well as a love of porcelain, is a consideration, then it is always better to collect a series that is not particularly in favour. There is no knowing how fashions will change, but at least the collector will be able to even out the costs overall. This is not to say that it is necessary to set one's sights on a large collection, for Kaendler and his assistants were commercially minded enough to realize that not everybody could afford or would want a large series, so they made the figures as complementary pairs or even able to stand alone. This was done in such a way that gestures were made within a pair, but at the same time turned inwards again, so that each figure is complete in itself. Although they often used engravings to give them inspiration, the figures were re-created in the round and show no sign of their two-dimensional origins. The King and his ministers gave Meissen porcelain as presents to visiting dignitaries because it was considered rarer and finer than gold. If this enormous esteem were translated into present day monetary values, then eighteenth-century Meissen porcelain is underpriced today.

Of course it is impossible to show in one book every figure and group made in Meissen from 1731 to 1760, and we must apologize for certain personal preferences, but this we put down to our own form of porcelain malady. We count ourselves lucky that a fair proportion of the pieces shown have passed through our hands over the years, which has made antique dealing for us, as for many of our fellow dealers, a wonderful way of life rather than just a way of making a living.

*   *   *

Measurements, except where stated otherwise, refer to the height of figures.

Court Life

Eighteenth-century European aristocracy were greatly influenced by the French Court. Their favourite pastimes were hunting, masquerades and the theatre, both amateur and professional. The theatricals undertaken by members of the Court were part of the social calender, and provided an escape from the rigidly formal way of life. At other times this escape manifested itself in their dressing up as romanticized shepherds and shepherdesses, much as Marie Antoinette played and sprinkled perfume on her porcelain flowers. All things French were fashionable, and there was no aristocratic family that did not have French tutors and governesses and speak French.

The so-called Meissen 'Crinoline' and Court groups are full of romantic and exquisite gestures of tenderness; their embraces and clasped hands are all signs of lovers, but above all they are expressions of eighteenth-century sentiment. The peculiarly Meissen decoration on the skirts of the crinolined ladies gives the impression of silk brocade swinging as if in time to a Mozart minuet.

Although most of the groups are taken from engravings and paintings, some are Kaendler poking gentle fun at the many court romances and scandals, probably at the instigation of some malicious member of the Court, for without doubt as an artisan, even with the title of Model Master, Kaendler would only have been an onlooker at all court activities.

Hunting in eighteenth-century Saxony was strictly reserved for the aristocracy, as it was in most European countries. In Saxony, however, it was little more than the ritualized slaughter of wild animals, who were driven into a clearing to be shot by both men and women. With this in mind, it is not so surprising to find so many of the women in the hunting groups dressed in elaborate crinoline gowns. Hunting in Saxony was therefore very different from that in England, which invariably meant a country gentleman tearing across a field on a horse, chasing a fox; but perhaps the following rhyme applies to both, but in very different ways:

> 'Hunting's an old and honourable Sport,
> Loved in the country, and esteemed at Court,
> Healthful to the body, pleasing to the eye,
> And practised by our old Nobility'.

On many of the Meissen Court groups there will be found a pug dog. This dog, a popular breed in the eighteenth century, was also the insignia of 'The Order of the Pug Dogs', a sham Freemasons' Society. The Freemasons' Society originated in the medieval guilds of working masons who, because they went from job to job, had signs and gestures to admit them to their lodges (huts on working sites). Later the lodges became associations, and as early as 1646 a lodge admitted members who were not working masons, and so developed lodges of 'speculative' masons. From the beginning of the eighteenth century masons held their 'lodge' meetings in coffee houses and taverns, presumably in private rooms, as such places were frequented by every kind of person, from those of high standing in the community to pimps and thieves, and the more unlawful customers would surely have interfered with these meetings.

In the middle of the eighteenth century, however, the Pope decreed that Freemasonry was to be outlawed. This caused great distress to the Saxon aristocracy, for although they were devout Catholics, they greatly enjoyed the social aspects of Freemasonry. They therefore invented their own society, 'The Order of the Mops' (pug dog), kept those parts of Freemasonry that would not offend the Pope, and added further refinements such as the inclusion of women in the society. Thus we get many groups with allusions to Freemasonry that include women and pug dogs.

Figures similar to those illustrated in this chapter may be found in the following museums:

Bayerisches Nationalmuseum, Munich, Germany.
British Museum, London, England.
Capo di Monte Castle, Naples, Italy.
Fitzwilliam Museum, Cambridge, England.
Musée des Arts Décoratifs, Paris, France.
Musée de Dijon, France.
National Museum, Stockholm, Sweden.
The Residenz, Ansbach, Germany.
Villa Floridiana, Naples, Italy.
The Wadsworth Atheneum, Hartford, Connecticut, USA.

Lovers at a Spinet.
Model by J.J. Kaendler, c.1741/2.
9 inches wide.
Meissen records show that Kaendler considered this a difficult group to produce.

Freemason.
Model by J.J. Kaendler, c.1740. 12 inches.
Extremely finely decorated courtier with all the accoutrements
of Freemasonry: trowel, dividers, apron. The finely executed
paintings on the columns depict scenes with Freemasons.

The Seller of Hearts.
Model by J.J. Kaendler, c.1738. 8 inches wide.
This scene has been attributed to various court romances, but
is more likely to have been taken from a painting of a scene at
the Comédie Française in Paris. The trinket seller and the boy
servant in the background also appear as single figures.

Lovers with a Birdcage.
Model by J.J. Kaendler, c.1734. 7 inches wide.
Wonderful example of Kaendler's baroque style, especially where the man's feet extend beyond the base of the group.

Lovers with a Table.
Model by J.J. Kaendler, c.1734. 7 inches wide.
The same group as Lovers with a Birdcage but with the latter replaced by a table laid with a chocolate pot, two cups and saucers, and a sugar bowl. This use of the same group with alterations to make it look entirely new illustrated Kaendler's adaptability.

Freemason.
Model by J.J. Kaendler, c.1750.
12 inches.
There is a slight difference to the
Freemason on page 18 shown in the
angle of the hand holding the scroll of
paper and the trowel replaced by
dividers; the most obvious difference
is that the painted scenes have been
replaced by gilt scrolls and marbling.

OPPOSITE
Dame of the Order of the Mops.
Model by J.J. Kaendler, c.1745/50.
11 inches.
This figure represents the replacement
society for the outlawed Freemasons.

Lovers Kissing.
Model by J.J. Kaendler, c.1744. 8 inches.
Beautiful crinoline dress decorated with Indian flowers to simulate
brocade. This dress was called an andrjan, a loose garment of the rococo
period with a distinctive pleat at the back originating from Paris. This
group was inspired by a painting by François Boucher of a scene from a
Molière play.

Tyrolean Trinket Seller.
Model by P. Reinicke and J.J. Kaendler, c.1740. 6 inches.
Reinicke has adapted Kaendler's figure from The Seller of Hearts on page
18 to make this figure.

Lovers with Pug Dog.
Model by J.J. Kaendler,
c.1745. 4½ inches.
Small group with a favourite
theme of lovers and their dog.

RIGHT
Lady with Spaniel.
Model by J.F. Eberlein, c.1750.
7 inches including ormolu.
Unusual to find a spaniel dog.

FAR RIGHT
Gentleman with Hound.
Model by J.F. Eberlein, c.1750.
7 inches including ormolu.
This figure clearly shows
Eberlein's distinctive modelling
of slightly oriental eyes.

OPPOSITE
Sedan Chair with Two Porters.
Model by P. Reinicke, c.1750. 4½ inches.
The chair itself is decorated in the rococo style, and it is
interesting to see that the woman has a small dog on her lap.

Busts of Two Children.
Models by J.J. Kaendler, c.1753. 9 inches.
These busts are the only known figures produced at Meissen in
the eighteenth century with blue eyes. This was at the express
order of Augustus III, whose grandchildren they were.

Prince Louis Charles de Bourbon (1751–1761) and Princess
Marie Zepherine de Bourbon (1750–1755) were the two eldest
children of Louis, Dauphin of France (1729–1765), and Maria
Josepha of Saxony (1731–1767). Sadly the young prince, who
was idolized by his parents and grandparents, died of tubercular
bone disease at the age of 9, a tragedy from which his parents
never recovered, although they had 12 children altogether. They
both died within a few years of his death, and it was accepted at
the time that they had died of 'broken hearts'.

OPPOSITE
Elizabeth of Russia.
Model by J.J. Kaendler, c.1750. 11 inches.
Queen Elizabeth of Russia in full dress uniform wearing the
Order of St Andrew, with a young blackamoor servant boy
running beside the horse. A large amount of porcelain was
produced at Meissen for the Russian Court, both figures and
serviceware.

Elizabeth of Russia.
Model by J.J. Kaendler, c.1750. 11 inches.
This is almost identical to the plate on page 25, except for the absence of the blackamoor servant.

BELOW LEFT
Woman with Cat.
Model by J.J. Kaendler and P. Reinicke, c.1748. 5½ inches.
It is unusual to have a cat on a Meissen group.

BELOW
Man with Pug Dog.
Model by J.J. Kaendler and P. Reinicke, c.1748. 5½ inches.
Pug dogs were extremely popular in the eighteenth century, and this gentleman seems very proud of his dog and is demonstrating its ability to sit up and beg.

Dancing Master.
Model by J.J. Kaendler, c.1745.
7 inches.
His exaggerated dancing attitude
definitely suggests a dancing master.

Children playing.
Model by J.J. Kaendler, c.1760.
6 inches.
Finely dressed children playing with
mother's jewel-box. This group is
sometimes known as 'The Lottery'.

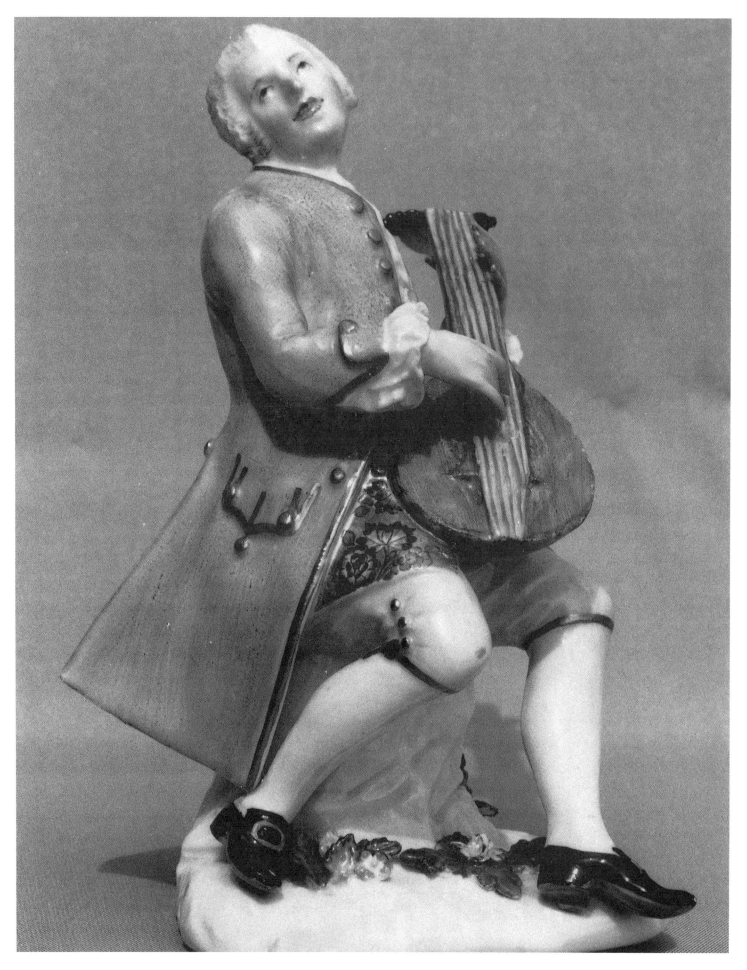

OPPOSITE
Mandolin player.
Model by J.J. Kaendler,
c.1750. 5½ inches.
A professional court musician
or an amateur musician.

Child musicians.
Model by J.J. Kaendler,
c.1755. 7 inches.
Inscription on music reads
'Sonata Cinquième Adagio'.
This piece particularly
illustrates that the figures were
made for the table and not
cabinets, as it can be viewed
from all sides equally well.

Polish Handkiss.
Model by J.J. Kaendler, c.1744. 9 inches without ormolu.
Poles and Saxons were very closely allied. Polish life fascinated the Saxons and there were many marriages between the two nationalities.

Polish Noblewoman.
Model by P. Reinicke, c.1750. 5 inches.
The sleeves on the jackets of both the Polish men and women are very distinctive.

OPPOSITE
Miniature Hunting Figures.
Model by J.J. Kaendler and P. Reinicke, c.1750. 2½ inches.
Hunting figures are extremely prolific in Meissen, but these miniature figures are particularly charming.

Lady with Bird's nest.
Model by J.F. Eberlein,
c.1748. 9 inches.
This lady is obviously in
hunting dress but seems to
be fascinated by the contents
of the bird's nest.

1
1 Lady with Sheep.
Model by J.J. Kaendler, c.1755. 5½ inches.
At first glance this lady appears to be a shepherdess, but this is belied by her fine clothes and
shoes; she is obviously once again a lady playing. Her hat looks to have been made of green
straw, but the strange spotting of the colour was caused by burning in the kiln, known as
'orange-peel', a common fault with green.

II

III

IV

TOP LEFT
II Barn with Hunters.
Models by J.J. Kaendler and P. Reinicke, c.1750. Barn 4½ inches high and hunters 2½ inches high.
The barn comes from the same set as No. 28 made for Count Brühl, and is one of the items mentioned specifically in the inventory of his porcelain after his death.

ABOVE
III Skaters.
Model by P. Reinicke, c.1755. 5½ inches.
An elegant couple about to go skating. The shape of the eighteenth-century ice skates is interesting.

IV Dancer.
Model by J.J. Kaendler, c.1755. 6 inches.
An elegant example of the rococo style.

V

VI

V Hunting Pair.
Model by J.F. Eberlein, c.1745. 6 inches.
Although these two figures are dressed in matching colours, they
are not a pair, as the colours on the bases differ.

TOP RIGHT
VI Pair of Falconers.
Model by J.F. Eberlein, c.1746. 7 inches.
Falconry was a favourite sport in Europe in the eighteenth century,
as exemplified by the following:
> 'The Pheasant Cock the woods doth most frequent,
> Where Spaniels spring and perch him by the scent,
> And when in flight the Falcon with quickened speed,
> With Beak and savage talons makes him bleed.'

VII Hunter with Dog.
Model by J.F. Eberlein, c.1745. 5½ inches.
A good example of Eberlein's work, especially the dog.

VII

X Hussar on Horseback.
Model by P. Reinicke, c.1755. 8 inches.
This figure is also in miniature form.

VIII Hunter.
Model by J.J. Kaendler, c.1745. 5½ inches.
Wonderful stance of a man pointing a rifle,
probably inspired by a painting by Ridinger.

OPPOSITE LEFT
XI Drum Major on Horseback.
Model by P. Reinicke, c.1750. 7 inches.
This figure was made as a table salt, as the
drums are hollow.

OPPOSITE RIGHT
XII The Blown Kiss.
*Models by J.J. Kaendler, c.1740. 5½ inches
high.*
This pair is extremely unusual in that the
figures are made free-standing without
stumps or bases. The lady has free-formed
petticoats under her skirt. The decoration is
in sgraffito, obtained by cutting away part of
the overlaying colour to expose a contrasting
colour below. These were inspired by an
engraving by Filloueul from a painting by
J.B. Pater.

IX Duellists.
Models by J.J. Kaendler, c.1755. 8 inches.
One of the most expressive pairs of figures
known. The aggression on the face of the
man in green and the fear on the face of the
man in white is amazing.

Duels arose from the practice of 'Trial by
Battle' of medieval times, but were already
being frowned upon in the eighteenth
century. Later they were outlawed, but seem
to have persisted until the end of the
nineteenth century. The abolition of the duel
was lamented by some, as it was argued that
'the dangers of being called out demanded
and cultivated carefulness of speech and
courtesy of manners, which imposed some
checks on conduct'.

X

XI

XII

XIII **Shepherd Boy playing Bagpipes.**
Model by J.J. Kaendler, c.1750. 4½ inches.
Group inspired by drawing by Boucher.
See also the etching, page 54.

See also the etching, page 54.

OPPOSITE LEFT
XV **Milkmaid.**
Model by P. Reinicke, c.1750. 5 inches.
A milkmaid on her way to market.

OPPOSITE RIGHT
XVI **Peasant.**
*Model by J.J. Kaendler and J.F. Eberlein, c.1748.
4½ inches.*
This is possibly the little jester Christophe Kirshe,
companion to Joseph Fröhlic, who also appears dressed
in Harlequin clothes decorated with playing cards.

OPPOSITE RIGHT
XVII **Shepherdess and Cavalier.**
*Model by J.J. Kaendler, c.1745.
7 inches.*
The cavalier appears to be making
overtures to the shepherdess!
Although her dress is fairly rustic,
she is wearing shoes.

OPPOSITE LEFT
XVIII **Pair of Gardeners.**
*Model by F.E. Meyer, c.1750.
7 inches.*
The gardening tools at the back of
this group are unusual and
interesting. Note that he has flowers
and she has vegetables, presumably
as her interests lie in the kitchen.

XIV **Peasant's Barn with Doves.**
*Model by J.G. Ehder, c.1750.
5 inches.*
This barn comes from the set of
houses and cottages made by Ehder
for Count Brühl as a table-centre,
and presumably modelled on a
village known to both the Count and
Ehder. On the Count's death, it was
found that he had sixty-seven of
these little porcelain houses.

XIII

XV

XVI

XVII

XVIII

TOP LEFT
XIX **Peasant taking Snuff.**
Model by J.J. Kaendler, c.1740. 5½ inches.
Strong baroque modelling.

ABOVE
XX **Beggar Peasant Musician.**
Model by J.J. Kaendler, c.1740. 5 inches.
Note the wonderful feeling of despair on this figure's face, and the
early sgraffito decoration on the bottom of the skirt.

XXI **Cherry Pickers.**
Model by J.J. Kaendler, c.1755. 12 inches.
Charming group inspired by a painting by Jacopo Amiconi.

Soldiers.
Models by P. Reinicke and J.J. Kaendler, c.1745.
4¹/₂ inches.
The two soldiers on the left are dressed in Electoral
uniform.

House.
Model by J.J. Kaendler, c.1750. 12 inches.
This house is from the celebrated village made for
Count Brühl. This large and exceptionally fine house
was probably one of the houses occupied by the Count
himself, as most of the houses in this set are peasant
cottages.

Miniature figures of Hussars.
*Models by P. Reinicke and J.J. Kaendler,
c.1750. 2½ inches.*
These miniature horsemen were made at
the orders of King Frederick of Prussia as
a present for the son of Queen Elizabeth
of Russia.

**Miniature figure of a Man on
Horseback.**
*Model by P. Reinicke and J.J. Kaendler,
c.1750. 2½ inches without mounts.*
This figure is unusually made as a
perfume bottle. The head of the man
comes away to reveal a hollow body to
hold the perfume. The base is mounted
in gold with a mirror underneath. Travel
in town and country in the eighteenth
century was dangerous, and it was
common for the traveller to be armed
with some form of firearm. Then, as
now, it was extremely unlikely for a rider
to achieve any accuracy with a hand-gun
while on the move, and therefore a rifle
was invariably carried, or more probably
a type of blunderbuss.

OPPOSITE
Lovers.
Model by J.J. Kaendler, c.1750. 7 inches.
Gentleman offering a posy to a lady
playing a mandolin. At first sight these
are a shepherd and shepherdess, but this
is belied by their dress, and in face and
dress they are almost identical to the
Lovers with Pug Dog, page 23.

Augustus III.
Model by J.J. Kaendler and J.F. Eberlein, c.1740. 9 inches.
This figure, in the white, shows the King in Polish costume and wearing the Order of the Golden Fleece. The statue was made to the order of Count Brühl. The figure is based on a painting by the court painter Louis Sylvestre, who lived at the Saxon Court between 1715 and 1750.

The Housekeeper.
Model by J.J. Kaendler, c.1760. 6½ inches.
The housekeeper is poring over her account books with an account on her knees, surrounded by bottles.

Miniature figures of a Man and Woman with Muffs.
Models by J.J. Kaendler and P. Reinicke, c.1750. 2½ inches.

Miniature figure of a Woman with a Dog.
Model by P. Reinicke and J.J. Kaendler, c.1750. 3 inches.
This figure is a perfume bottle and the head of the dog comes off. Even though this is a miniature, the modelling clearly shows the weight of the dog resting on the woman's hip.

FAR RIGHT
Miniature figure of a Gentleman.
Model by P. Reinicke, c.1750. 3 inches.
This figure has a gold-mounted vinaigrette base.

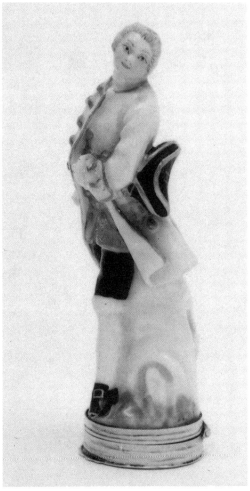

Country Life

The peasant figures illustrated in this chapter show not only Kaendler's ability to work in the baroque style, but his uncompromising way of showing the truth. In some of these figures you can see the harshness of peasant life in the early eighteenth century, not only by the raggedness of their clothes but often in a look of almost despair on their faces, which further confirms Kaendler's genius as a modeller and master of porcelain.

Later in the eighteenth century, however, when the rococo French style became popular, Kaendler and the other modellers completely altered their modelling and so encompassed the so-called 'Dresden Shepherdess' which for years was how Meissen figures were described in the English-speaking world.

Although Kaendler and his assistants did make many shepherds and shepherdesses, they were not quite the bland, simpering models so popular in the nineteenth century and so infamous in the twentieth century. Many of the shepherd groups were taken from drawings by artists such as François Boucher, and these, of course, were drawn for French society, where only enough realism was wanted to make the sentimental idyll credible. The aim was to offer an escape from the harsh realities of life, as had been shown by Kaendler in his earlier figures, and to ward off any suspicions that such a thing as a revolution by the populace might some day take place; and although these shepherds and shepherdesses are not as bland as those of the nineteenth century, there is a general smoothing away of the hollows under the cheekbones of the earlier figures, and the clothes become pretty, even if sometimes the figures are barefoot.

Figures similar to those illustrated in this chapter may be found in the following museums:

Bayerisches Nationalmuseum, Munich, Germany.
Bernisches Historisches Museum, Bern, Switzerland.
Capo di Monte Castle, Naples, Italy.
Fitzwilliam Museum, Cambridge, England.
Museo Capitolino, Rome, Italy.
Museum für Kunst und Gewerbe, Hamburg, Germany.
Museum of Art, Providence, Rhode Island, USA.
Smithsonian Institution, Washington, D.C., USA.
Villa Floridiana, Naples, Italy.
The Wadsworth Atheneum, Hartford, Connecticut, USA.

Shepherd playing a Flute.
Model by P. Reinicke and J.J. Kaendler, c.1750. 5 inches.
This truly is a shepherd, playing his flute to while away the time
whilst tending his sheep with his dog.

Shepherdess.
Model by J.J. Kaendler and P. Reinicke, c.1750. 5 inches.
Charming shepherdess gathering flowers.

Peasant Shearing a Sheep.
Model by J.J. Kaendler, c.1750. 7 inches.
This figure is an extremely good example of using a drawback
of porcelain to advantage. The tree stump which is usually used
to support the figure has been used for the shepherd to sit on,
making it appear to be a necessary part of the figure.

Pair of Shepherd Lovers.
Model by J.J. Kaendler, c.1750. 5 inches.

Dancing Shepherdess.
Model by P. Reinicke, c.1750. 5 inches.

Shepherdess and Cavalier.
Model by J.J. Kaendler, c.1750. 6 inches.
Romantic group of a cavalier capturing the pretty shepherdess in a rope of flowers.
Inspired by a drawing by François Boucher.

Listener at the Well.
Model by J.J. Kaendler, c.1750.
8 inches.
Different version of shepherdess and cavalier with a rope of flowers. A listening intruder is hiding behind the wall. Inspired by an engraving of a drawing by François Boucher.

Engraving of a drawing by François Boucher of the *Listener at the Well*.

OPPOSITE
Pair of Children holding Chickens.
Model by P. Reinicke and J.J. Kaendler, c.1750. 4½ inches.

Shepherd with Bird's nest.
Model by J.J. Kaendler, c.1755.
8 inches.
Good modelling of simple shepherd clothing.

OPPOSITE
Girl with Open Basket.
Model by P. Reinicke, c.1755.
5 inches.
Made as a table salt.

Etching from a drawing by François Boucher of *Shepherd Boy Playing Bagpipes. See also* plate XIII, page 38.

Drunken Fisherman.
Model by J.J. Kaendler, c.1740.
5½ inches.
This very humorous figure with the fish coming out of holes in the man's shirt is typical of Kaendler's sense of fun. The marks on the figure are where the glaze has missed and dirt has penetrated the porcelain.

Piedmontese Bagpiper.
Model by J.J. Kaendler, c.1745.
9 inches.
Taken from an engraving by J. Dumont.

54

Dancing Dutch Peasants.
Model by J.J. Kaendler, c.1745.
7 inches.
Taken from a painting by Teniers.

Beggar Musician.
Model by J.J. Kaendler, c.1740.
5 inches.
One of several versions of this
theme.

Gypsy.
Model by J.J. Kaendler, c.1748. 15 inches.
This figure cannot in any way be called pretty. The face, warts and all, looks as if it must have belonged to somebody Kaendler had seen, probably among a band of gypsies wandering through Meissen.

TOP LEFT
Dancing Peasants.
Model by J.F. Eberlein, c.1748. 5 inches.
From a drawing by Jean-Antoine Watteau.

Etching of a drawing of *Dancing Peasants* by Watteau.

Dancing Peasant.
Model by J.J. Kaendler, c.1740. 5½ inches.
Probably the companion figure to plate XIX, page 40.

Farmer scattering Seed.
Model by P. Reinicke, c.1748. 4 inches.

Religion

For hundreds of years artists have depicted scenes from the Bible in paintings and statues, and so it was only natural that orders would flood into the Meissen factory for porcelain figures of the Holy family, the Apostles and saints, to be displayed in chapels and private houses.

Kaendler made some large figures of the Apostles in the early 1730s. They were not always successful, however, for as with the large animals, they suffered from large firing cracks and not many seem to have survived. In 1736 and 1737 Kaendler made a slightly smaller set with much greater success, but the various religious figures made in the early 1740s were the most successful of all.

When Augustus II decided to enlarge the Japanese Palace (formerly known as the Dutch Palace), he ordered life-sized figures of the Apostles, a peal of bells, an altar, a pulpit, an organ and a throne, the principal parts of which were to be made in porcelain.

Orders for religious figures were constantly received from people such as Cardinal Albani, Pope Clement XII, and the Dowager Empress Wilhelmina Amalia, the mother of Queen Maria Josepha.

It is amazing that Kaendler, the son of a Protestant pastor, was able to produce figures more aligned with the Catholic faith than his own, although he did convert to Catholicism later in life. Whether this was a political move or through conviction is not known.

Figures similar to those illustrated in this chapter may be found in the following museums:

Bayerisches Nationalmuseum, Munich, Germany.
British Museum, London, England.
The High Museum, Atlanta, Georgia, USA.
The Hermitage, Leningrad, USSR.
Victoria and Albert Museum, London, England.

OPPOSITE
Crucifixion Group.
Models by J.J. Kaendler, c.1750. 14 inches to tip of Cross.
Corpus Christi group with the Virgin Mary and Mary Magdalene, shown with original leather travelling case.

Engraving of *Corpus Christi* by Jacques Callot.

Jesus Carrying the Cross.
Model by J.J. Kaendler, c.1740. 18 inches.

Engraving of *Jesus Carrying the Cross* by Jacques Callot.

St Peter.
Model by J.J. Kaendler, c.1736.
18½ inches.
Part of the first successful series of Apostles
made by Kaendler with gold decoration.
The crossed keys to heaven were adopted as
symbol of the papacy.

St Peter.
Model by J.J. Kaendler, c.1745. 10 inches.

St Jacob.
Model by J.J. Kaendler, c.1740. 10 inches.

OPPOSITE
St Mark the Evangelist.
Model by J.J. Kaendler, c.1740. 10 inches.
The figures of the Apostles were inspired by engravings of
Bernini's Apostles. St Mark became the patron saint of Venice.

OPPOSITE
St Nepomuk.
Model by J.J. Kaendler, c.1742.
14 inches.
St Nepomuk was Father Confessor to the
Empress. It is said that it was he who
coined the phrase 'Death Before
Dishonour', when he was asked to reveal
the contents of the Empress's
confessions. Because he refused, he was
thrown into the Danube and drowned.

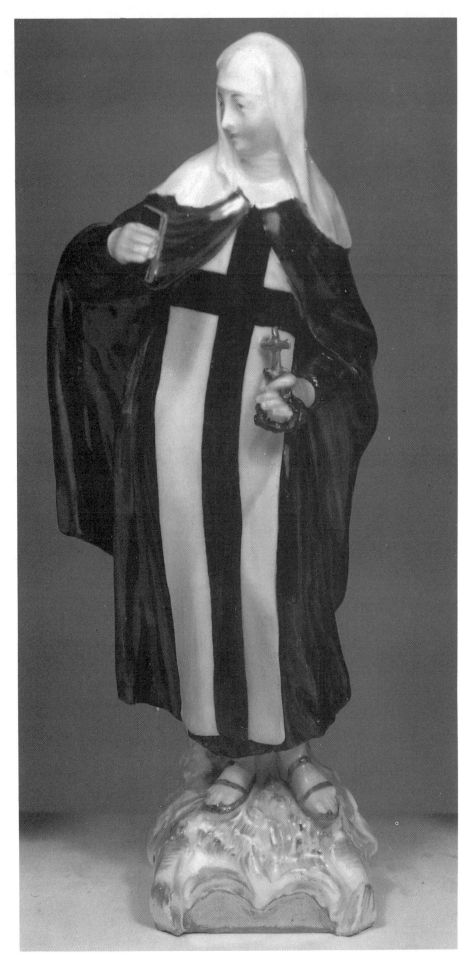

Nun.
Model by P. Reinicke and J.J. Kaendler,
c.1750. 7 inches.
A figure of a nun from the Order of St
John. St John of God founded the
Hospitallers in 1539, which became
famous for introducing a more
sympathetic approach to nursing. He
was the patron saint of hospitals and the
sick.

Monk.
Model by J.J. Kaendler, c.1745. 6 inches.
Behind the monk on the ground is a bishop's mitre
which has led experts to suggest that this is another
version of St Nepomuk.

St Bridget.
Model by J.J. Kaendler and P. Reinicke, c.1760.
7 inches.
Born of a noble Swedish family, St Bridget was
married before the age of 15 to a Swedish prince. The
marriage lasted 28 years and she bore him 8 children.
When widowed, she founded a monastery in
Waldstena in 1344 which was to be known as the
Holy Order of the Most Holy Saviour.

Monastery Provender.
Model by J.J. Kaendler, c.1760. 3 inches.
This figure was made as a perfume bottle. The monk's head is
removable as the stopper. He is carrying a basket of eggs and a
fowl, and smuggling a young woman in a sheaf of corn! The
monastic way of life, with its genuine search for holiness and peace,
has frequently been interrupted through the centuries by
penitential struggles to subdue the demands of the flesh.

Mythology

Mythology is the study of religious or heroic legends so foreign to a student's experience that he cannot really believe them to be true. Hence the English adjective 'mythical', meaning incredible; and also the omission from standard European mythologies of all Bible narratives, even when closely parallelled by myths.

The educated men of the eighteenth century were fully conversant with Greek mythology. Illustrated editions of Ovid's *History of the Gods* were widely known. J.J. Kaendler, as the son of clergyman, had a good education with a strong classical grounding, as was usual with the middle and upper classes of the time. Add to this the vast amount of classical statues in the parks and palace, together with the paintings featuring classical mythological scenes in the royal collection, and it will be understood why he and his assistants produced so many models in this genre.

It was also fashionable at that time to put contemporary events and people into classical garb, especially royalty, thereby portraying them as equal to the ancient gods, without offending their Christian beliefs. For five years Kaendler worked on a model of Augustus III as a Roman emperor seated on a rearing horse of more than life size. Although the project was very dear to his heart, it was never fully completed.

Kaendler was in his element when creating, with his assistants, little Cupids in all sorts of poses and guises. They are boldly and humorously conceived, and were extremely popular at the time, both as individual figures and as part of larger groups. Unfortunately tastes change, however, and they and to a large part all mythological subjects, are not as popular in the late twentieth century. This is a great pity, as they are frequently wonderful examples of porcelain sculpture.

Similar figures to those illustrated in this chapter may be found in the following museums:

The Hermitage, Leningrad, USSR.
Musée des Arts Décoratifs, Paris, France.
Museum für Kunst und Gewerbe, Hamburg, Germany.
Museum für Kunsthandwerk, Frankfurt/Main, Germany.
National Museum, Stockholm, Sweden.
Palazzo Conservatori, Rome, Italy.
Victoria and Albert Museum, London, England.
Villa Floridiana, Naples, Italy.

OPPOSITE
Pan and Syrinx.
Model by F.E. Meyer, c.1750.
8 inches.
Pan, although born with the legs, horns and beard of a goat, must not be confused with the satyrs. The word 'Pan' meant 'all', as the sight of Pan amused all the immortals on Olympus. Pan's reed pipe represented Syrinx, who was changed into a set of reeds by her father, to save her from the attention of Pan.

Allegory of Music.
Model by J.J. Kaendler, c.1755. 11½ inches.

Allegory of Earth.
Model by J.J. Kaendler, c.1745. 6½ inches.

Allegory of Fire.
Model by J.J. Kaendler, c.1745. 7½ inches.

Allegory of Marriage.
Model by J.J. Kaendler, c.1760. 7½ inches.

XXII **Pilgrim.**
Model by P. Reinicke, c.1750. 5 inches.
A courtier dressed for a pilgrimage.

XXII

XXIII Church.
Model by J.G. Ehder. c.1742. 14 inches without ormolu mount.
This church was made as part of the village of houses for Count Brühl. The metal trees are set with Meissen porcelain flowers.

XXIII

XXIV

XXV

XXIV Apollo in a Grotto.
Model by J.J. Kaendler and P. Reinicke, c.1755. 12 inches.
Amongst other things, Apollo was King of the shepherds,
and frequently depicted with a shepherd's crook. His most
celebrated sanctuary was a deep cavern in Delphi.

XXV Rape of Prosperine.
Model by J.J. Kaendler, c.1750. 9½ inches.
Prosperine was carried away by Hades, King of the
Underworld. This is a particularly good example of
Kaendler's art, showing his knowledge of anatomy and his
ability to go beyond the normally accepted limitations of
sculpture in porcelain.

XXVI

XXVI **Satyress and Child.**
Model by J.J. Kaendler, c.1755. 7 inches.
Satyrs, both male and female, represented the elementary spirits of the
forests and woods, whose appearance would terrify shepherds and travellers.
But they really only loved pleasure and good cheer.

XXVII **Allegory of Sound.**
*Model by J.J. Kaendler & P. Peinicke,
c.1760. 8 inches.*

XXVII

XXVIII
XXVIII Vegetable Saleswoman.
Model by J.F. Eberlein, c.1745.
7 inches.
This figure has an unusual straw hat,
presumably to protect her from the
sun when working on her vegetable
patch. Although this was made in the
1740s, the colouring is more to the
rococo taste. The vegetable in her left
hand appears to be celery which,
although known in Roman times, was
not properly cultivated in France until
the sixteenth century.

TOP RIGHT
XXIX Street Musician.
Model by J.F. Eberlein, c.1750. 7 inches.

XXIX

XXX Map Seller.
Model by J.J. Kaendler, c.1748.
7 inches.
Prints and maps of different nations
appear on several versions of this figure.
Kaendler has elaborated on the original
drawing by Bouchardon.
See also the drawing, page 93.

XXX

Europe.
Model by J.J. Kaendler, c.1746. 7 inches.
Made as one of the four continents, with royal crown, sceptre and orb. On the base are a globe
showing Europe, a book with geometrical signs, and a protractor.

Chronos.
Model by J.J. Kaendler, c.1745. 14 inches.
Representing Time, and used a watch holder. Kaendler also carved a similar figure to this in stone as a funerary monument.

Four Large Greek Mythology Groups.
Models by J.J. Kaendler, c.1760. 13 inches.
Apollo and Minerva; Chronos and Antonia; Diana and Alexander; Bacchus and Diana.

Clio.
Model by J.J. Kaendler, c.1748. 10 inches.
The Muse of history. Her attribute was the heroic trumpet.

Apollo.
Model by J.J. Kaendler, c.1748. 10 inches.
Apollo is shown as the god of music with his lyre and the archer god with a quiver of arrows.

OPPOSITE
The Labours of Hercules.
Model by J.J. Kaendler, c.1755.
21 inches including ormolu base.
Hercules was the personification of
strength. The founding of the ancient
Olympic Games was attributed to him.

**Aeneus Rescuing his Father Anchises
after the Fall of Troy.**
Model by J.J. Kaendler, c.1755.
10½ inches.

Thalia.
Model by J.J. Kaendler, c.1740. 18 inches including ormolu base.
Thalia, the Muse of comedy, is seated on an ormolu base holding the mask of comedy in one hand and a boy dressed in Italian comedy Harlequin clothes in the other.

Urania.
Model by J.J. Kaendler, c.1740. 18 inches including ormolu base.
Urania, the Muse of astronomy, is seated on an ormolu base with the accoutrements of her science: telescope, celestial globe, calipers; her blue cloak is painted with stars.

Apollo Playing a Lute.
Model by J.J. Kaendler, c.1747.
13½ inches.
Part of a large group centred
around Mount Parnassus.

**Venus and Cupid Riding in a
Chariot drawn by Two
Rearing Horses.**
Model by J.J. Kaendler, c.1755.
12 inches.

Bacchus and Cupid with a Candlestick.
Model by J.J. Kaendler, c.1755. 10 inches.
Bacchus, or Dionysus, was the god of wine and the god of vegetation. He was also used to represent the season 'Autumn'.

Cupids in Disguise.
Models by J.J. Kaendler, c.1755. 4 inches.
Examples from numerous figures of Cupids dressed as mortals. These are a Money Lender, an Actor, a Peasant, and a Pastry Seller.

Jason and Medea.
Model by J.J. Kaendler, c.1745. 5½ inches.
Medea, who fell in love with Jason, was a skilful magician. She showed him how to overcome the difficulties imposed upon him before he could seize the Golden Fleece.

Boreas and Oreithyia.
Model by P. Reinicke and J.J. Kaendler, c.1750. 9 inches.
A similar figure to that of plate XXV, page 74, but without Kaendler's original concept of the woman across the man's shoulders, and therefore not such an exciting model. Oreithyia was the daughter of Erichthonius, the King of Athens. She was seen by Boreas whilst she was playing on the shore; he promptly carried her off and married her.

Europa and the Bull.
Model by F.E. Meyer, c.1750. 8½ inches.
Europa was the daughter of Agenor, King of
Tyre. Zeus fell in love with Europa. Taking the
form of a beautiful white bull, he wandered
among the herds that Hermes had driven down
to the seashore where Europa was playing. He
looked so gentle munching a crocus that the girl
felt safe with him and eventually climbed on his
back. Before she knew what was happening, the
bull was swimming towards Crete.

Pair of River Gods.
Model by J.J. Kaendler, c.1744. 8 inches wide.
These figures were inspired by an engraving of
the Grenelle Fountain in Paris, designed by
Edmé Bouchardon.

Bacchus and Two Putti.
Model by J.J. Kaendler, c.1750. 11 inches.
Bacchus, here shown as a youth, was the King of Viniculture
and had festivals dedicated to him. Having found how to make
wine from grapes, he at first drank without moderation, but
later went to an oracle to cure himself. When cured, he
undertook long journeys across the world in order to spread the
inestimable gift of wine amongst mortals.

Pair of Putti Riding Dolphins.
Model by J.J. Kaendler, c.1750. 5 inches.

Street Traders

In the eighteenth century the large European cities were filled with men and women calling out their wares in a jargon which had come down to them almost entirely unchanged from the Middle Ages. The earliest mention of the London cries was in the fourteenth century by John Lydgate, a monk of the Benedictine Abbey of Bury St Edmunds and a friend of Chaucer. These cries are still known in the form of nursery rhymes and songs; they give an insight into daily life on the streets in the seventeenth and eighteenth centuries. On all sides the strident voices of traders and beggars were to be heard creating a discordant din. The cries were innumerable, and little if any attempt was made for peace and quiet, for in Paris alone there were some 20,000 water carriers. Although the lives of these people may seem strange, it was often to their liking, as conveyed by this eighteenth-century ditty:

'I am a lusty beggar,
And live by others giving.
I scorn to work,
But by the Highway lurk,
And beg to get my living;
I'll in the wind and weather,
Wear all ragged garments,
Yet, though I'm bare,
I'm free from care,
A fig for high preferments!'

The early history of the street traders is obscure, whereas the circumstances which necessitated their existence are obvious. The poor city pedlars earned their living mostly by catering for their own class; to cry their wares was their only form of advertising. It is reasonably certain that these people were illiterate, with the exception of course of the ballad sellers, although even they may have sung out their wares by hearsay. In contrast, there must have been some who were numerate in order to count their wares, such as 'At a groat a peck each oyster worth tuppence', and 'Four for sixpence – mackerel'.

Throughout history, artists have recorded street traders and workmen in all forms, as it gave them the chance to portray faces where character had been hewn the hard way. According to the great eighteenth-century artist, de la Tour, 'Every human being has had to bear to a greater or lesser extent the burdens proper to his status. These leave their mark in a more or less pronounced way. The important thing is to know first of all how to seize upon this, so that when you have to paint a king, a general, a priest or a porter, these people reflect their position as much as possible.'

Today we are fortunate not only to have in our museums the engravings and paintings of the eighteenth century, but also the wonderful figures made at Meissen by Kaendler and his assistant modellers of the street traders, most of which were taken from drawings by such artists as Bouchardon, Marcellus Laroon, Boucher, Watteau and Hüet.

Although in some ways these series of street traders fall into two categories, the baroque and rococo, we have split them up even further by showing from which engravings they were taken and also separated them by size.

During our research, particularly into the London street traders, we have been able to discover that those drawn by Marcellus Laroon were specific individuals living in the centre of London, which gives us an insight into the quality of life on the streets of London in the eighteenth century.

Although this has been of particular interest to us as Londoners, we hope that it may encourage someone else to delve into the history of some of the Paris traders depicted by Edmé Bouchardon, whose drawings also show individual character.

Paris Street Traders of the Baroque Period

[*Illustrated on pages 93–103*]

These figures modelled by J.J. Kaendler and J.F. Eberlein were frequently inspired by engravings by the Comte de Caylus of drawings by Edmé Bouchardon. They are interesting not only because they enabled Kaendler and Eberlein to produce figures in the baroque style, but also because they show more character in the faces than those of the later rococo-style figures taken from drawings by Christophe Hüet. These drawings were probably done from life in much the same way as the London Criers by Marcellus Laroon, French artists as far back as the fifteenth century have been fascinated by the people of the streets, but with the advent of so much book printing in the eighteenth century, these prints would have been known right across Europe, particularly in the Saxon Court, where all things French were so popular.

Figures similar to those illustrated in this chapter may be found in the following museums:

The Ashmoleon Museum, Oxford, England.
Bayerischen Nationalmuseum, Munich, Germany.
British Museum, London, England.
The Hermitage, Leningrad, USSR.
Musée des Arts Décoratifs, Paris, France.
Museum of Art, Providence, Rhode Island, USA.
Museum für Kunst und Gewerbe, Hamburg, Germany.
Smithsonian Institution, Washington, D.C., USA.
Victoria and Albert Museum, London, England.
Wadsworth Atheneum, Hartford, Connecticut, USA.

Paris Street Traders of the Rococo Period

[*Illustrated on pages 104–125*]

Kaendler was ordered by the King to travel to Paris in the early 1750s to accompany a large porcelain mirror which was to be a present to the King's daughter, Maria Josepha, on her wedding to Louis, Dauphin of France. This mirror was more than nine feet tall, was decorated with figures such as Apollo and Polyhymnia flower wreaths and foliage, and had a full-sized table attached, all made in the full rococo style.

During Kaendler's time in Paris he visited the main Meissen dealer, by name J. Hüet. This dealer had a brother, Christophe Hüet, an Académie drawing master and an artist of some repute, who was commissioned by Kaendler to produce designs for a series of Cries of Paris that could be executed in the rococo style. These drawings are still in the Meissen archives, but although it has been thought that the characters were drawn from life, this seems doubtful, as so many of them resemble drawings of similar subjects by Boucher, Watteau and other artists working at that time; and although Christophe Hüet produced several famous works, such as that hanging in the museum of Nantes, these drawings appear to be fairly unusual for him.

From 1737 on, at first annually and then every other year, large exhibitions of art were held in Paris. Salons as they were called, after the Salon Carré in the Louvre, where they were held. On these occasions the Academicians, themselves almost all the major artists of the day, exhibited their works. These Salons formed the artistic ideas of the rococo style. At that time there were neither museums nor collections open to the public, and therefore the Salons provided an invaluable opportunity for artists such as Hüet to see other artists' work.

The majority of this series were modelled by Peter Reinicke, although in some instances it is possible to see the guiding hand of Kaendler. These small figures, mostly 5 inches high, are predominately decorated in the delicate rococo colours of pale pink, green, turquoise and beige, with gilded scrolling bases. Some of the figures are shod in shoes, but most have sabot (clogs), which were not only cheaper for these extremely poor street people to buy, but easier to wear on the cobbled streets of eighteenth-century Paris.

Not all the Paris street traders modelled in the rococo style can be traced to Hüet drawings. Some were inspired by engravings of Boucher and Watteau drawings, and some were created by the modellers themselves in the same style.

London Street Traders

[*Illustrated on pages 126–137*]

The figures of this series were in the most part modelled by J.J. Kaendler, with some help from Peter Reinicke, in a mixture of the rococo style with the scrolling bases and with more than a backward glance at the baroque in the strength of the character modelling in the faces. Kaendler drew inspiration for these models from the engravings by Pierce Tempest of Captain Marcellus Laroon's drawings. Laroon was the son of a Dutch painter and lived in London during the time of Hogarth, who was a great friend. He was obviously something of an adventurer, having been a singer at Covent Garden, an actor, and a soldier who served in Flanders and Spain, and when in London, he was frequently turned out of Drury Lane taverns and carried before the Justices for being drunk and disorderly. This side of his life would explain how he was able to draw the portraits of such people as the pimp known as the 'Squire of Alsatia' in the thieves' den area of London. What is particularly interesting about these figures is that they represent people notorious enough to have had their names and occupations recorded in contemporary records; but although they had great appeal for Kaendler, the Meissen records show that he was not aware that these were portraits of actual people and used the titles at the base of the engravings.

In the eighteenth century the great canal system of England was developed which made it easier for peasants and craftsmen to come into London to sell their wares. In the London of that time merchandise of almost every description was carried and cried in the streets, as shops were little more than open shanties in the poorer parts of the town, which made the street traders with their baskets of wares greatly in demand. From very early times the criers, particularly the broad sheet sellers, were the carriers of news to an illiterate people and were amongst the few people to move about freely. As in Paris, one wonders about the noise. A certain Ralph Crotchett of London described the clamour in a letter to the *Spectator* on 18 December 1711 offering his services as Comptroller General for the Cries of London, presumably without success. He referred to the 'Twanking of pots and pans and the sow gelder's horn' and said that London appeared to be 'a distracted city'. He quoted a match seller who was so raucous that a potential customer paid him to stay off his street. What a surprise when the next day all the match sellers in the neighbourhood came to his house hoping to be paid off too!

The different streets and squares were known for the different foods sold in each area.

> 'Thames Street gives cheeses; Covent Garden Fruits;
> Moorfields old books, and Monmouth Street old Suits.'

These sadly are disappearing; even the famous Covent Garden fruit and vegetable market has moved south of the River Thames. Similar shops and trades, however, do still seem to congregate in the same areas: book dealers near the British Museum, art dealers at St James's and tailors in Savile Row.

In the seventeenth and eighteenth centuries, however, the greatest gatherings of street sellers were at the fairs. These were usually held for one day at a time on open spaces, and the populace could buy everything they could possibly want, and watch jugglers, musicians and all the various street performers of the day. The most famous of all fairs, dating from medieval times, was the Bartholomew Fair, held in London's Smithfield (now the meat market) on St Bartholomew's day, the 24th August.

In 1742, Ranelagh Gardens opened in London. A contemporary observer wrote: 'The gardens were filled with tents and marquees. In one corner stood a maypole and people were dancing round it to the music of the tabour and pipe and all were masked. All round the outside of the amphitheatre were shops or booths filled with Dresden (Meissen!) china, japan (lacquer) etc. and all the shop keepers in masks. Booths were set for gaming, men were selling wine and tea, and about 2000 people were present. However, the chief amusement of Ranelagh was the promenading round the circular area of the Rotunda to see and be seen.' One can imagine the Squire of Alsatia and his Courtesan with her mask were frequent visitors to Ranelagh.

The cries of the London street traders have been handed down to us in the form of songs and nursery rhymes such as 'Cherry Ripe' and 'I met a Pieman Going to the Fair'. This particular rhyme seems to allude to the famous John Sharpe England, immortalized in a drawing by Hogarth, who was known for his delectable pies and his immaculate dress. In London we still buy our fruit and vegetables from street traders or 'costermongers', which is a term derived from the days when they sold the old 'Costard apples'.

> 'Let None Despise,
> The Merry Merry Cries
> Of Famous London Town.'

Russian Street Traders

[Illustrated on pages 138–143]

These figures are loosely adapted from engravings of drawings by Jean-Baptiste Le Prince, a student of Boucher who went to Russia to make a record of the costumes and ways of the Russian people in the eighteenth century. The manners and customs of the French aristocracy were adopted by the Russian Court, and an Academy of Art was founded. However, they felt that there was little local talent, and funds were made available for an exchange of art students between France and Russia.

To travel large distances in the eighteenth century was always a hazardous occupation, particularly as far as from Paris to Russia. Le Prince made this journey partly by road and partly by boat, and it was during the sea passage that his ship was captured by Corsicans. Being an artist early in his career, Le Prince probably had little in the way of valuables and so was able to continue his journey. However, he must have had connections of high standing as he was presented to the Tsar when he was in St Petersburg. This journey, and his stay in Russia with its terrible winters, must have weighed heavily on a man already suffering poor health. Nonetheless, he produced a large portfolio of drawings of Russian life which gave him great critical success on his return to Paris.

Le Prince was also generally acknowledged to have invented the aquatint process and patented it in 1768. His poor health finally gave way, and he died at the age of 47 in 1781.

The harshness of the Russian climate tends to produce a hardy physique, and because of the limited seasons, the peasant has learnt to work in outbursts in order to cultivate and gather his crops. This is quite clearly portrayed in Le Prince's drawings, but Peter Reinicke has not shown this, probably because he did not understand clearly whom the engravings showed, and the figures are unusually stiff for Meissen of this period.

Drawing of the *Map Seller* by Edmé Bouchardon.
See also plate XXX, page 76.

ABOVE
Laundry Man.
Model by J.J. Kaendler, c.1748. 7 inches.
This is a very good example of Kaendler's baroque art, with a strong emphasis on the modelling and very little colour. The facial features are particularly well copied from Bouchardon's drawing. Such a nose had to belong to somebody real. This man was an itinerant washer-man who called at the house to do laundry, bringing his own cauldron to boil the wash and his own flat iron.

Drawing of the *Laundryman* by Edmé Bouchardon.

Drawing of *Porter* by Edmé Bouchardon.

Porter.
Model by J.J. Kaendler, c. 1748. 7 inches.
Here Kaendler has added to the original drawing with
a piece of luggage on the carrier. The lack of
decoration shows the strong baroque modelling.

Drawing of *Fife and Drum Player* by Edmé Bouchardon.

Fife and Drum Player.
Model by J.J. Kaendler, c.1748. 7 inches.
Strong modelling indicates the loud noise from banging that drum.

Drawing of *Bread Boy* by Edmé Bouchardon.

Bread Boy.
Model by J.J. Kaendler, c.1748. 7 inches.
The sullen look on the boy's face in the drawing has not been
repeated by Kaendler, probably for commercial reasons, but he
has been able to suggest the weight of the basket of bread.
Bakers in Paris in the eighteenth century were strictly controlled
and not allowed to sell bread until they had served a long
apprenticeship. Each day's baking had to be sold before
4 p.m., or if after that at a greatly reduced price. In 1710 there
were fifteen bread markets in Paris where over a thousand
bakers sold their produce.

Drawing of *Hurdy Gurdy Player* by Edmé Bouchardon.

Hurdy Gurdy Player.
Model by J.J. Kaendler, c.1748. 8 inches.
These street musicians were reputed to have come from as far away as Provence, where presumably life was even harder than in Paris.

Trinket Saleswoman.
Model by J.J. Kaendler, c.1750. 7½ inches.
Companion figure to the Trinket Salesman, but of a slightly later date.

OPPOSITE
Bird Seller.
Model by J.J. Kaendler, c.1748. 7 inches.
The bird sellers from each period and each city always appear to have happy smiles on their faces. The sale of singing birds was a common sight, but the noise the birds made, mixed with the salesman's cry, must have produced quite a raucous sound.

TOP LEFT
Trinket Salesman.
Model by J.J. Kaendler, c.1748. 7½ inches.
The only apparent deviation from Bouchardon's drawing is that Kaendler has the man pointing to his wares in the box rather than with his hand tucked into his coat. The careful modelling of the buttons and scissors in the box is a delight, as it gives an insight into the haberdashery of the eighteenth century.

Drawing of *Trinket Salesman* by Edmé Bouchardon.

OPPOSITE
Chicken Saleswoman.
Model by J.J. Kaendler, c.1748. 7½ inches.
A strong, peasant, hard-working face with no attempt to make her look pretty.

Grape Salesman.
Model by J.J. Kaendler, c.1750. 5 inches.
This figure shows the man selling his grapes from the basket usually worn on the back when picking the grapes. Grapes could be brought to Paris in a fresh state by cutting the bunch when not quite ripe, leaving a section of stem which was immersed in a bottle half-filled with water.

Pair of Vegetable Sellers.
Model by J.J. Kaendler, c.1750. 5 inches without ormolu bases.
This pair of figures was also made with empty baskets as table salts, and with baskets with plain pierced tops to take flowers.

Beggarwoman with Children.
Model by J.J. Kaendler, c.1748. 7 inches.
This group was inspired by a painting by Daulle. Beggars in Paris were supposed to be either blind or infirm, but a comment made at the time was, 'There seemed to to an extraordinary amount of blind persons begging who got around as if seeing with their feet'.

Vegetable Salesman.
Model by J.F. Eberlein, c.1745. 7 inches.

Old Woman Selling Fruit.
Model by J.J. Kaendler, c.1748. 7½ inches.
This figure was repeated several times, but with different produce in her basket.

Farmer with Goat.
Model by J.J. Kaendler, c.1746. 7½ inches.
The spotting on this figure was caused by irregular glazing, and dirt has got into the unglazed biscuit porcelain over the years. The peasant features of this man are well defined. Goat's meat was usually eaten when the kid was between 6 weeks and 3 months old; after this it became too tough and the goat was then kept for milk. This trussed up kid was obviously to be sold for meat.

Flower Seller.
Model by P. Reinicke, c.1757. 5 inches. Design by Christophe Hüet.

> 'Come buy my fine roses, my myrtles and stocks;
> My sweet smelling balsams and close growing box.'

Café Waiter.
Model by P. Reinicke, c. 1757. 5 inches. Design by Christophe Hüet.
By 1754 there were fifty-six cafés in Paris selling coffee which could be consumed on the premises or delivered elsewhere for 2 sous including sugar.

Waffle or Pastry Seller.
Model by P. Reinicke, c.1757. 5 inches. Design by Christophe Hüet.

Pieman.
Model by P. Reinicke, c.1757. 5 inches. Design by Christophe Hüet.
Hot and cold pies were a common delicacy in every city in Europe in the eighteenth century, and are still a very popular snack in England. The term 'pie' was originally derived from 'magpie': just as the bird collects assorted objects, so the dish had assorted ingredients.

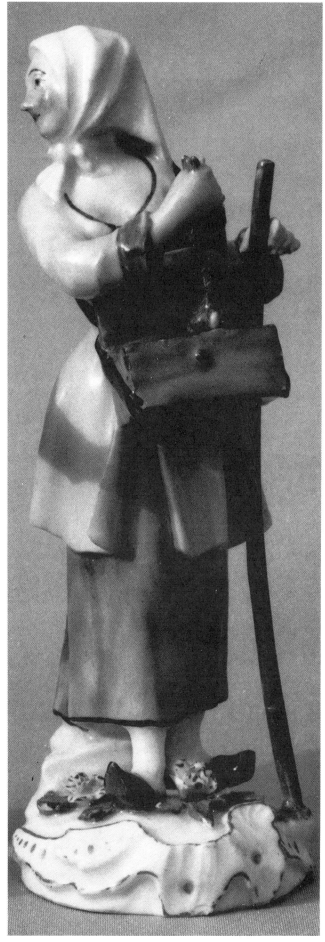

Tisane or Lemonade Seller.
Model by P. Reinicke, c.1757. 5 inches.
Design by Christophe Hüet.
Tisane was a lemon or herbal drink sold
both hot and cold.

LEFT
Marmot Girl.
Model by P. Reinicke, c.1757. 5 inches.
Design by Christophe Hüet.
This girl was probably a Savoyard. The
marmot was an animal found high in the
French Alps, similar to a rabbit or hare,
but larger and very fierce. The girl's
marmot was not for sale, but exhibited
for reward as a curiosity.

Herb Seller.
Model by P. Reinicke, c.1757. 5 inches.
Design by Christophe Hüet.
Herb sellers would gather their produce
from the hedgerows outside the city.

'Come by my mint, my fine green mint,
    here's lavender for your clothes;
Here's parsley and winter savory and
    heartsease which all do chose.'

Drawing of a *Turkey Cook* by Christophe Hüet. *See also* plate XXXI, page 109.

Chicken and Egg Seller.
Model by P. Reinicke, c.1757. 5 inches.
Design by Christophe Hüet.

'Buy my young chickens or a fowl well fed;
And we'll not quarrel about the price;
'Tis thus I get my daily bread;
As all the year round my fowls are nice.'

Grape Seller.
Model by P. Reinicke, c.1757.
5 inches. Design by Christophe Hüet.
One of the few street traders who actually has scales to weigh his produce.

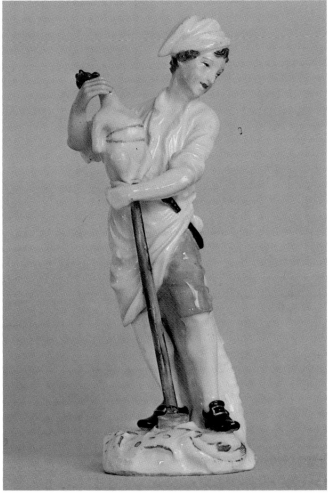

XXXI

XXXII

XXXIII

TOP LEFT
XXXI Street Cook with a Turkey.
Model by P. Reinicke, c.1757. 5 inches.
Design by Christophe Hüet.
A seventeenth-century English jingle reads:
> 'Turkeys, heresy, hops and beer,
> Came to England all in one year.'
This may not have been too accurate, but the first turkey was
mentioned by Archbishop Cranmer in 1541.
See also the drawing, page 108.

ABOVE
XXXII Peepshow Man.
Model by P. Reinicke, c.1757. 5 inches.
Design by Christophe Hüet.
One of the most popular of all street criers, and one of the very few
licensed to trade at night. Frequently seen in paintings of festivals
and masquerades.

XXXIII Beggarwoman with Baby.
Model by P. Reinicke, c.1757. 5 inches.
Design by Christophe Hüet.

XXXIV Flute Player.
Model by P. Reinicke, c.1757. 5 inches.
One of the street musicians.

BELOW LEFT
XXXV Flower Girl.
Model by P. Reinicke and J.J. Kaendler, c.1755. 4 inches.
Inspired by an engraving of a drawing by Boucher, but the modellers have added the basket of flowers held by the girl in the background.
See also the engraving, page 123.

BELOW
XXXVI Flower Girl or Courtesan.
Model by P. Reinicke and J.J. Kaendler, c.1755. 5 inches.
From the rather arch expression on this girl's face, we may assume that she probably practised two trades. This extra activity on the part of young flower girls was greatly suspected by the authorities in the eighteenth and nineteenth centuries.

XXIV

XXXV

XXXVI

XXXVII Meat Salesman.
Model by P. Reinicke, c.1750. 4 inches.
It is to be presumed that it is meat beneath the white cloth, as this boy has a knife under one arm, and wears a shirt of the traditional butcher's blue and white stripes and a rather hygienic-looking cap on his head.

BELOW
XXXVIII Lemon Seller.
Model by F. Meyer, c.1755. 5 inches.
This model is very evocative of Meyer's style in the rococo manner. He made a small series of these Paris criers which was not taken directly from drawings by Hüet, as those by P. Reinicke had been. These figures were also made in the larger size of 7 inches.

BELOW RIGHT
XXXIX Waffle or Pastry Seller.
Model by F. Meyer, c.1755. 5 inches.
This is from the same series as the Lemon and Waffle Sellers.

XXXVII

XXXVIII

IXL

XL
XL Tisane or Lemonade Seller.
Model by F. Meyer, c.1755. 5 inches.
This is from the same series as the Lemon Seller.

Lemon Seller.
Model by P. Reinicke, c.1757. 5 inches. Design by Christophe Hüet.
Orange and lemon sellers are probably the street traders which most readily come to mind, for who does not remember Nell Gwynne.

'Fine Sevill Oranges; Fine Lemons Fine;
Round, sound, and tender, inside and rine;
One Pin's prick their vertue show;
They've liquor by their weight, you may show.'

Oublieux Man (Lotterie).
Model by P. Reinicke, c.1757. 5 inches. Design by Christophe Hüet.
On payment of a sou, the hands of the dial on the drum on his back were spun and a sweetmeat was the prize. One of the few street traders in Paris to be licensed.

Chicken Plucker.
Model by P. Reinicke, c. 1757. 5 inches. Design by Christophe Hüet.
All manner of services were performed on the streets as well as the selling of wares.

Street Cook.
Model by P. Reinicke, c. 1757. 5 inches. Design by Christophe Hüet.
It was cheaper and easier to take your food to a street cook rather than keep a fire going in a poor household. However, it looks as if a large amount of tasting went on by this corpulent gentleman.

The Courtesan.
Model by P. Reinicke, c.1757. 5 inches. Design by Christophe Hüet.
Companion to the Marquis, although one does not know whether the wistful expression on her face was to attract attention or show her feelings for her lifestyle.

The Marquis.
Model by P. Reinicke, c.1757. 5 inches. Design by Christophe Hüet.
A fancy name for a fancy gentleman, who was in fact a pimp.

Drawing of *The Marquis* by
Christophe Hüet.

ABOVE RIGHT
Vinegar Salesman.
Model by P. Reinicke, c.1757.
5 inches. Design by Christophe Hüet.
Vinegar was of prime importance
before refrigeration for pickling and
preserving meat, eggs and vegetables
during shortages in winter. Therefore
it is not surprising to see the man
pushing such a large barrel around, in
comparison to the small amount of
wares the other street traders carried.
It is a most interesting piece in this
series because of the difficulty it posed
of complying with the lightness of the
rococo, but at the same time giving
the impression of the heaviness of the
barrel.

Drawing of *The Fishseller* by Christophe Hüet.

OPPOSITE

White Radish Seller.

*Model by P. Reinicke, c.1757. 5 inches.
Design by Christophe Hüet.*
These large white radishes were a
common vegetable in the eighteenth
century.

'White Radish, white round lettuce
    white;
You hear me cry, Come Mistress buy;
Make my burden light.'

Nightwatchman.

*Model by P. Reinicke, c.1757. 5 inches.
Design by Christophe Hüet.*
The nightwatchman lit your way to your
home late at night and would also sell
you liquor, or a drink intended to bring
sobriety to the inebriated. This was
known as 'saloop', a cure unknown to us
now. It was considered a sovereign cure
for drunkeness by the young bloods of
the eighteenth century and by all
accounts was quite pleasant to drink.
Although at first sold by these
nightwatchmen, it eventually found its
way into the taverns and coffee houses of
the time. The ingredients of this beverage
were herbs such as sassafras and cuckoo-
flowers. There does not appear to be any
mention of this drink after 1860.

Fish Seller.

*Model by P. Reinicke, c.1757. 5 inches. Design
by Christophe Hüet.*
Fish was brought up the Seine to Paris on
barges and sold at the market. These women
called out 'Live Carpe – all fresh'. This would
have been a doubtful claim, as they were only
allowed to buy their fish late in the day after the
servants from the richer households had picked
it over earlier.

Oyster Seller.

*Model by P. Reinicke, c.1757.
5 inches.*
Oysters were eaten mostly by the poor
until this century.

'New oysters, new oysters at a groat
    a peck,
Each oyster worth tuppence,
Fetch bread and wine that we
    may eat;
Let us lose no time with such
    good meat;
A banquet fit for a prince.'

Drum and Fife Player.
Model by P. Reinicke, c.1757. 5 inches.
Design by Christophe Hüet.
The noise of the street musicians added to that of the cries of the traders must have been deafening. The drum is an ancient instrument introduced during the Crusade.

OPPOSITE
Ballad Seller.
Model by P. Reinecke, c.1757. 5 inches.
Design by Christophe Hüet.
Although this man is playing the fiddle, this was to attract attention in order to sell the ballads he kept in the pouch tied around his waist.

   'Songs, songs, beautiful songs,
     Love songs, newest songs, popular
       songs;
     Songs three yards a penny.'

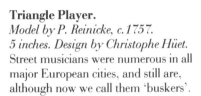

Triangle Player.
Model by P. Reinicke, c.1757.
5 inches. Design by Christophe Hüet.
Street musicians were numerous in all major European cities, and still are, although now we call them 'buskers'.

Drawing of the *Fife and Drum Player* by Christophe Hüet.

Hurdy Gurdy Player.
Model by P. Reinicke, c.1757. 5 inches. Design by Christope Hüet.
Although street musicians still abound in the streets of Paris and London, hurdy gurdy players are seldom seen now, but this instrument must have been very popular in the eighteenth century, as we see it being played by many figures in porcelain. This instrument was known in England as a 'hum-strum'.

Mandolin Player.
Model by P. Reinicke, c.1757. 5 inches.
One of the street musicians.

Street Singer.
Model by P. Reinicke, c.1757. 5 inches.

Vegetable Seller.
Model by P. Reinicke, c.1758. 4 inches.

Engraving of the drawing of *The Flower Girls* by
François Boucher.
See also plate XXXV, page 110.

See also plate XXXV, page 110.

OPPOSITE
Winter Vegetable Seller.
Model by P. Reinicke, c. 1760. 4 inches.

Egg Seller.
*Model by P. Reinicke, c.1757. 5 inches. Design by
Christophe Hüet.*
The large pot on her head may have held cream or
pickled eggs.

123

Town Crier.
Model by P. Reinicke, c.1757. 5 inches. Design by Christophe Hüet.

Cheese Seller.
Model by P. Reinicke, c.1757. 5 inches. Design by Christophe Hüet.
On her head she holds a tray of small pots of fresh unfermented cheese of a type that is now known as Petit-Suisse or home-made cheese, a very creamy unsalted cheese made from whole milk with cream added. Contrary to its name, this cheese was first made in Normandy which, of course, is not a great distance from Paris.

OPPOSITE
Potted Flower Seller.
Model by P. Reinicke, c. 1757. 5 inches.

       'All – a – growing; All – a – blooming.'

Fruit Seller.

Model by J.J. Kaendler, c.1750. 5 inches.

This figure shows Kaendler making a token nod to the
fashionable rococo by including the scrolling base under
a strong figure with no pretence towards prettiness. A
true London costermonger with his 'kerchief round his
neck, apart from his knee breeches and long coat, he is
dressed not unlike the present-day costermongers. The
drawing is entitled 'Any Bakeing Pears', which were
large, very hard pears known as Wardens grown in
most country gardens.

> 'Just fresh from the tree;
> All you who have money;
> Come buy them of me.'

Etching of *Fruit Seller* by Pierce Tempest from a drawing by
Marcellus Laroon.

Etching of *Ballad Sellers* by Pierce Tempest of a drawing by
Marcellus Laroon.

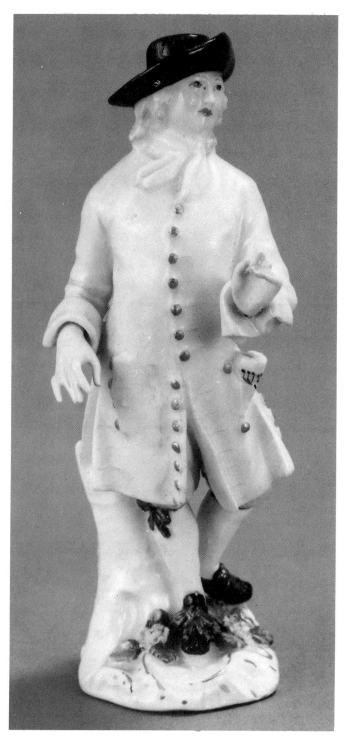

Ballad Seller.

Model by P. Reinicke, c.1750. 5 inches.

This pretty little lady's name was Mrs Parker, and she was one of the numerous people selling ballads and broadsheets in London at that time. Their activities made them notorious enough to produce the following rhyme.

> 'Let not the Ballad Sellers shrilling strain;
> Amid the swarm thy listening ear detain;
> Guard well thy pocket, for these sirens stand
> To aid the labours of the diving hand;
> Confederate in the cheat, they draw the throng,
> And cambric handkerchiefs reward the song.'

The eighteenth-century poet William Shenstone wrote: 'The ways of the Ballad singers and the cries of the Halfpenny Pamphleteers appeared so extremely humorous from my lodgings in Fleet Street, that it gave me pain to observe them without a companion to partake. For alas, laughter is by no means a solitary entertainment.'

Ballad Seller.

Model by P. Reinicke, c.1750. 5 inches.

This man was Roger Teasdale, a companion to Mrs Parker.

Etching of *The Beggarwoman with Children* from a drawing by Marcellus Laroon.

Beggarwoman with Children.
Model by P. Reinicke, c.1750. 5½ inches.
Fine modelling shows the holes and raggedness of the clothes, but the romanticized rococo
makes itself felt.

The London Quaker.

Model by P. Reinicke and J.J. Kaendler, c.1750. 4 inches.

This figure and its companion are much smaller than the rest of the series but come from the same etchings and are portraits of real people. The man was John Kelsey, a Quaker dedicated to converting other people to his religion. This notion took him to Constantinople with the intention of converting the Grand Vizier to Christianity. Unfortunately, he did not realize that the local populace would not understand English, and was arrested for making a nuisance of himself. He was rescued by the English Ambassador, who agreed to allow the soles of Kelsey's feet to be beaten to release the madness from his soul before he was put on a ship bound for England. However, Kelsey escaped, tried once again to convert the local people to Christianity, and was re-arrested, bound in chains, and put onto another ship for England.

Etching of *The London Quaker* by Pierce Tempest from a drawing by Marcellus Laroon.

Sarah of Covent Garden.
Model by P. Reinicke, c.1750. 4 inches.
Companion to John Kelsey. It is not known whether she accompanied him to Constantinople.

Etching of *Sarah of Covent Garden* by Pierce Tempest from a drawing by Marcellus Laroon.

The Squire of Alsatia.
Model by J.J. Kaendler and P. Reinicke, c.1750. 5 inches.
Kaendler obviously did not realize who this was, as he gave him
a slight look of a gentleman. He was in fact a notorious pimp
who governed a thieves' den area of London known as Alsatia
after Alsace, which in the seventeenth century had been an
extremely troublesome part of Europe.

The London Courtesan.
Model by J.J. Kaendler and P. Reinicke, c.1750. 5 inches.
The companion to *The Squire of Alsatia*. Is her wistful
expression to beguil her customers or bewail her calling?

Etching of *The Squire of Alsatia* by Pierce Tempest from a
drawing by Marcellus Laroon.

Trinket Salesman.
*Model by J.J. Kaendler and P. Reinicke,
c.1750. 5 inches.*
This man's box contains a much more
crowded and varied collection of trinkets
than the original etching shows.

'Come Buy – Come Buy a Hornbook,
Why buys my pins and needles?
Such things do I in the City cry,
Of times to 'scape the Beadles,
Then I do cry,
Come Buy – Come Buy'

A Beadle was a parish officer appointed
by the local clergy to punish petty
offenders.

OPPOSITE
Etching of *Trinket Salesman* by Pierce
Tempest from a drawing by Marcellus
Laroon.

Money Lender.
Model by J.J. Kaendler, c.1748. 5½ inches.

Fish Seller.
Model by J.J. Kaendler, c.1750. 5 inches.
Fish sellers were numerous in all the cities of Europe. Fish was
consumed by the poor not just because it was cheaper than meat,
but as a custom left from the Early Christian church as a form of
abstinence; fish was thought to reduce the passions and meat to
stimulate them. Until the seventeenth century, special 'Fyssche
Days' were observed when Christians were obliged to go without
meat on Wednesdays, Fridays and Saturdays, and for the twenty
days of Lent. Mackerel were allowed to be sold on Sundays as this
fish was thought to be particularly perishable, although it is
doubtful whether any of these women's fish was very fresh. Their
cry was:

'Alive and Fresh, good herrings oh.'

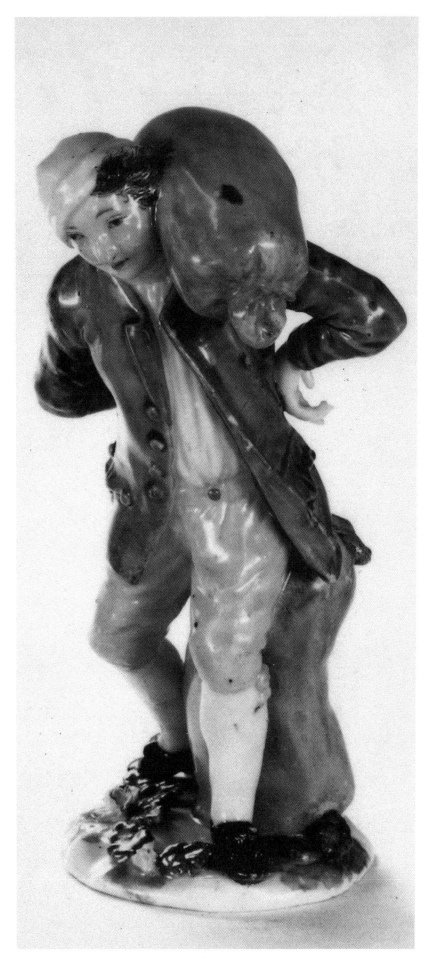

Etching of *Cherry Seller* by Pierce Tempest
from a drawing by Marcellus Laroon. *See also*
plate XLIII, page 146.

Coalman.
Model by P. Reinicke and J.J. Kaendler,
c.1750. 4 inches.

> 'Says Oyster Nan to Small Coal Tom;
> Come out of there you dirty honey;
> Tom very archly bites his thumb;
> Saying dirty hands will get clean money.'

Drinks Seller.
Model by P. Reinicke, c.1755. 5½ inches.
This man was probably selling a drink called 'Sbiten', a hot beverage made from honey and much more popular in Russia than tea or coffee.

OPPOSITE
Woman with Two Jugs.
Model by P. Reinicke, c.1755. 5 inches.
Note the fur lining to her coat, but this time more in keeping with local dress. She is probably selling water.

Etching of a drawing by J.B. Le Prince of Russian subjects.

Fish Seller.
Model by P. Reinicke, c.1755. 5½ inches.
The stiff posture is meant to convey that the man is balancing the bowl of fish on his head. It also serves to illustrate that whilst Reinicke was a master modeller in comparison with the rest of the world, he was not quite as creative as Kaendler when this figure is compared with Kaendler's London criers with baskets on their heads.

Milk Seller.
Model by P. Reinicke and J.J. Kaendler, c.1755. 5½ inches.
The posture of this figure has more movement than that of the Fish Seller.

OPPOSITE
Man with Stave.
Model by P. Reinicke, c.1755. 4 inches.
Small figure of a man striding along with a tall stave in his hand.

Pair of Figures with Firewood.
Model by P. Reinicke, c.1755. 4 inches.
The wood may have been for fires, or part of the celebration to
herald the coming of spring, when tree branches were placed
over the doorway after a long hard winter.

OPPOSITE ABOVE
Troika and Passengers.
Model by J.J. Kaendler, c.1755. 10 inches wide.
A rather liberal interpretation of the Le Prince drawing, but
very interesting in that the base is supposed to represent snow
with no rococo scrolls and no flowers. This group was also made
without the horse.

OPPOSITE
Etching of a drawing by J.B. Le Prince of Russian subjects.

Etching by Pierce Tempest from a drawing by Marcellus Laroon. *See also* plate XLI opposite, page 145.

Etching of *The Quack Doctor* by Pierce Tempest from a drawing by Marcellus Laroon. *See also* plate XLII opposite, page 145.

144

XLI

XLI **Bird Seller.**

Model by P. Reinicke and J.J. Kaendler, c.1750. 5 inches.
One of the instances when the modellers added fur to the costume, probably because the etching they had was not very distinct. Sellers of birds were popular throughout Europe.

> 'Why do you ask why I look so arch;
> My trade is at its height in March;
> Come! Buy your singing birds of me;
> And fill your house with harmony.'

See also the etching opposite, page 144.

XLII **The Quack Doctor.**

Model by J.J. Kaendler, c.1750. 5 inches.
This porcelain figure was extremely well interpreted into porcelain by Kaendler from Laroon's drawing. The man was a Dutchman named Hans Buling, known throughout London for his flamboyant seventeenth-century dress, worn to attract attention in order to sell his coloured waters as 'cure-alls'. The monkey was known in slang terms as a 'Jack Pudding', and also used as a crowd puller. Quacks used the coffee-houses in London to advertise their incredible cures for every known ailment.
See also the etching opposite, page 144.

XLII

XLIII **Cherry Seller.**

Model by J.J. Kaendler and P. Reinicke, c.1750. 5 inches.

A very faithful interpretation of Laroon's drawing. It is just possible to see the set of scales in the basket, but the purpose of sliding cherries on sticks is not known.

> 'Here's round and sound;
> Black and white cherries;
> Two pence a pound.'

Fruit sellers sold 'fresh fruit' when in season, but in the winter they sold nuts and dried fruits, which were mostly imported and probably gave little profit to the poor street traders. So we must presume that life in winter was particularly hard, not only from the harshness of the weather but also the lack of fruit to sell.

See also the etching on page 137.

XLIV **Tailor.**

Model by J.J. Kaendler, c.1750. 9 inches.

A master craftsman, probably a member of a guild judging by his dress. He appears to be showing a sample of cloth in his hand.

XLV

XLV Spinster.

Model by J.J. Kaendler, c.1750. 9 inches.

This lady carries two spindles of wool. What appears to be a shoe last under her arm is possibly a weaving shuttle with pointed ends carved out of wood.

TOP RIGHT

XLVI Seated Cook.

Model by J.J. Kaendler, c.1750. 6 inches.

Another street cook, although we can assume that the fire is not alight in his brick oven, as he is sitting upon it.

XLVI

XLVII The Lacemaker.

Model by J.F. Eberlein, c.1745. 5 inches.

This figure probably portrays the famous court lacemaker Barbara Uttman, whose portrait also appears on Meissen snuff-boxes. On her lap is a shape known as a lace-pillow, which gave the name of pillow lace to the particular kind of lace popular at that time. The lace was made by weaving plaited threads held on ivory bobbins. Henry III of France loved lace so much that he covered himself in cascades of it. James I of England complained that 'People are selling their estates to pay for it'. Barbara Uttman must have been held in great esteem to have had this figure made of her.

XLVII

XLVIII

XLVIII Dutch Fisherman.
Model by P. Reinicke, c.1750. 5 inches.
This man stands with his catch at his feet, but the peculiar attitude of his hands seems to be indicating 'the one that got away'.

XLIX The Pandur.
Model by J.J. Kaendler, c.1748. 9 inches.
This figure, armed to the teeth, is reminiscent of a present-day Afghanistan rebel.

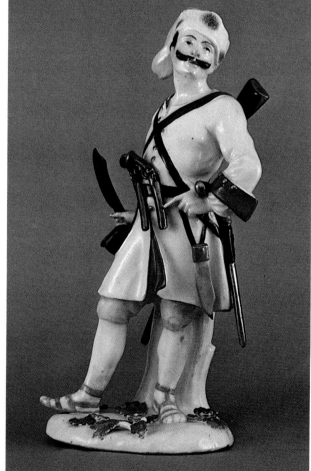

XLIX

L

L **Chinese Woman with a Child.**
Model by P. Reinicke, c.1750. 6 inches.
Inspired by an engraving by J.J. Balachou of a drawing by
François Boucher entitled *Les Délices de l'Enfance*.

TOP RIGHT
LI **Chinese Woman with Two Children.**
Model by P. Reinicke, c.1750. 6 inches.
Inspired by an engraving of a drawing by François Boucher
entitled *Les Délices de l'Enfance*.

LI

LII **Chinese Woman with Two Children.**
Model by P. Reinicke, c.1750. 5½ inches.
Inspired by an engraving of a drawing by François Boucher
entitled *Les Délices de l'Enfance*.

LII

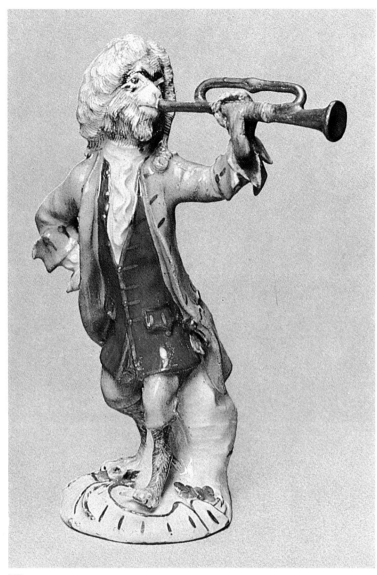

LIII

LIV

LV

LVI

LVII

LIX

LIX Columbine and Beltrame.
Model by J.J. Kaendler, c.1740. 7 inches.
This group is sometimes known as *The Spanish Lovers*.

LX Pulcinello.
Model by J.J. Kaendler and P. Reinicke, c.1745. 5½ inches.
This figure was made in various colour combinations and in
152   white, as here.

LX

Artisans

The series of workmen or artisans made by J.J. Kaendler in the middle of the 1750s, although not large in number, are of great interest to collectors, particularly in the twentieth century, for although some of the trades may have died out now, it is easy to identify their occupations. These figures give a great insight into the tools used in the eighteenth century. Although most of the figures were made in the rococo period, with the high scrolling bases of that time, the actual figures have the strength of the earlier period, and in no way try to cover up hard-working hands and muscles.

The importance of the mining community to the Saxon economy was periodically celebrated in court festivities. Figures of miners were made from engravings by Christoph Weigel to commemorate a festival at the Saxon Court in 1719 on the Planescher Ground, and even show the King dressed in miner's costume.

Figures similar to those illustrated in this chapter may be found in the following museums:

Bayerischen Nationalmuseum, Munich, Germany.
Cecil Higgins Museum, Bedford, England.
Fitzwilliam Museum, Cambridge, England.
The Hermitage, Leningrad, USSR.
Reiss-museum, Mannheim, Germany.
Villa Floridiana, Naples, Italy.

Wood Turner.
Model by J.J. Kaendler, c.1750. 9 inches.
From his dress we assume that this man was a master
craftsman and probably a member of a guild.

Blacksmith.
Model by J.J. Kaendler, c.1750. 9 inches.
The blacksmith was a hard-working member of any village,
where his services were of vital importance to everyday life.
OPPOSITE
Carpenter.
Model by J.J. Kaendler, c.1750. 8½ inches.
Note his long two-handled saw for cutting planks of wood from
trees, and the string tucked into his apron for giving him a
straight line. He also carries a short axe, probably for shaping
and cleaning the bark from the log.

Wheelwright.
Model by J.J. Kaendler, c.1750. 8 inches.
Like the blacksmith, this craftsman was essential to the community of the eighteenth century. The one here is seen chiselling into shape the hub of a large spoked wheel for a wagon or coach.

BELOW
Butcher.
Model by J.J. Kaendler, c.1750. 7 inches.
This figure appears to be falling over. This was an attempt by the modeller to emphasize the attitude of the butcher chopping through a bone. However, this became further emphasized when the figure slipped forward in the firing.

OPPOSITE
Seamstress.
Model by J.J. Kaendler, c.1750. 9 inches.
This woman carries a man's jacket sleeve over her right arm and in her hand she has a seam-splitting knife. The small piece of material in her other hand is presumably another part of the jacket.

Cook with Frying Pan.
Model by J.J. Kaendler, c.1745. 6 inches.
Many people took their food to a street cook rather
than have the expense of keeping a fire going
themselves.

OPPOSITE
Cook with Pan of Meat.
Model by J.J. Kaendler, c.1745. 6 inches.
The same model of a cook, but this time with a pan of
meat and with the addition of the brick oven.

Engraving of a woodcutter from a drawing by Edmé Bouchardon.

OPPOSITE
Woodcutter.
Model by J.J. Kaendler, c.1745. 5 inches.
This model was inspired by an engraving of a drawing by Bouchardon which shows a peasant
cutting up logs.

Tinker.
Model by J.J. Kaendler, c.1750.
5 inches.
This man mended pots and pans using a mobile stove for heating the lead with which he filled the cracks and splits. You can see clearly where he has mended the pot he is holding.

Coppersmith.
Model by J.J. Kaendler, c.1750. 5½ inches.
This craftsman would produce an article such as a cooking pot
from a sheet of copper, hammering it out just as a skilled panel-
beater works today.

Fisherman and Companion.
Models by J.J. Kaendler, c.1748. 6 inches.
The modelling of the fisherman's anatomy is an extremely fine
example of Kaendler's art. The muscles in the man's arms and
legs leave no doubt about a life spent in hard work. In contrast,
his female companion has the smooth oval face considered more
feminine in the eighteenth century.

King Augustus II dressed as a Miner.
Model by J.J. Kaendler, c.1750. 13 inches.
This figure was made as part of a table centre. The very fact
that the King is portrayed in a miner's ceremonial dress
shows the great esteem he had for his miners.

Mine Foreman.
Model by J.J. Kaendler, c.1750. 12 inches.
This man has an 'AR' monogram on his hat for Augustus
Rex, his king.

Miner working at the Mine Face.
Model by J.J. Kaendler, c.1750. 9 inches.
Miners in ceremonial dress.

Engraving of a miner by Christoph Weigel, after a watercolour by Frehling.

TOP LEFT
Miner Holding a Tray of Ore Samples.
Model by J.J. Kaendler, c.1750. 8 inches.

Miner working at the Mine Face.
Model by J.J. Kaendler, c.1750. 9 inches.

People from Distant Lands

The inhabitants and customs of the other side of the world fascinated Europeans. Expeditions were sent to the African continent, which apart from the terrible slave trade, also brought to Europe pictures of what seemed extremely exotic people, who were called 'Moors' or 'Blackamoors'. It was considered very fashionable to dress black servants in brightly coloured, fashionable clothes.

Inspiration for the Middle Eastern figures came from Jacques Le Hay's engravings of *Nations du Levant* commissioned by Charles de Ferriol, the French Ambassador to the Porte; and for the Chinese groups, from engravings of Boucher's drawings *Les Délices d'Enfance.*

Chinoiserie was an inherent part of the rococo, and people wanted everything depicting this far off exotic land, from porcelain to entire buildings, many of which have not survived the late eighteenth- and early nineteenth-century return to the so-called 'classical' style, so we are very lucky to have so many Meissen figures to give us an idea of the fashion of that time.

However, the fashion of decorating a surface solely for the sake of decoration is something that belongs to the West. For the Chinese artist, the placing and the spaces between are important in accordance with custom, legend, poetry and symbolism. The significance of this seems to have eluded even the earliest travellers to China such as Marco Polo, and it is not surprising to see 'German flowers' decorating the clothes of the Chinese figures and groups.

Figures similar to those illustrated in this chapter may be found in the following museums:

Bayerischen Nationalmuseum, Munich, Germany.
British Museum, London, England.
Capo di Monte Castle, Naples, Italy.
Cecil Higgins Museum, Bedford, England.
Fitzwilliam Museum, Cambridge, England.
The Hermitage, Leningrad, USSR.
Kunstgewerbemuseum, Cologne, Germany.
Musée des Arts Décoratifs, Paris, France.
Musée Nationale de Céramique, Sèvres, France.
Museum of Art, Providence, Rhode Island, USA.
Museum für Kunsthandwerk, Frankfurt/Main, Germany.
Villa Floridiana, Naples, Italy.
The Zwinger, Dresden, Germany.

The Horse Tamers.
Models by J.J. Kaendler, c.1750. 16 inches.
This pair of figures of a blackamoor and a
Turk holding white horses was inspired by
Guillaume Coustou's marble statue.

Sultan Riding a Rhinoceros.
*Model by J.J. Kaendler, c.1748. 9½ inches
wide.*
The model of the rhinoceros was inspired by
Durer's engraving.

Sultan riding on an Elephant.
Model by J.J. Kaendler, c.1748. 11 inches wide.

TOP RIGHT
Persian.
Model by J.J. Kaendler, c.1748. 8 inches.
This figure comes from a series modelled by Kaendler from engravings done by Le Hay of Paris in 1714. These were entitled *Receuil des cents estampes représentant les différentes Nations du Levant*. They were ordered by Monsieur le Comte Charles de Ferriol, French Ambassador to the 'Sublime Port', who, when first appointed to his post, refused to remove his sword as was usual in Islam when coming before the Sultan, on the grounds that it would tarnish the honour of his king. He was extremely lucky not to be executed for such an insult.

Engraving of *The Persian* done by Le Hay in 1714.

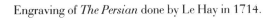

Turk.
Model by J.J. Kaendler, c.1748. 9 inches.
Inspired by engravings done by Le Hay in 1714 for the series
Nations du Levant.

Turkish Woman.
Model by J.J. Kaendler, c.1748. 9 inches.
From the series *Nations du Levant.*

169

OPPOSITE
The Amorous Turk and Companion.
Modelled by J.J. Kaendler, c.1745.
7 inches.
Inspired by an engraving of a drawing by François Boucher.

The Greek Musicians.
Models by J.F. Eberlein, c.1748–50. 8 inches.
These figures were inspired by an engraving of a drawing by Watteau.

Engraving of a drawing of a Greek musician by Jean-Antoine Watteau. Several hundred engravings of drawings by Watteau and Lancret were ordered by Count Hennicke, a high government official, in 1741, and put at the disposal of the Meissen modellers.

Turkish Man Holding Bowl.
Model by J.F. Eberlein, c.1746. 6 inches.
This figure was made as a table salt for Count Brühl.

Turkish Woman Holding a Bowl.
Model by J.F. Eberlein, c.1746. 6 inches.
This figure was made as a table salt.

Albanian.
Model by J.J. Kaendler, c.1748. 9 inches.
Inspired by an engraving done by Le Hay in 1714.

Chinese man with Child.
Model by P. Reinicke, c.1750. 6½ inches.
Inspired by an engraving of a drawing by François Boucher
entitled *Les Délices de l'Enfance*.

OPPOSITE
Turkish Woman.
Model by P. Reinicke, c.1748. 5 inches.

175

Chinese Couple Sitting in an Arbour.
Model by P. Reinicke, c.1755. 7 inches.
Inspired by an engraving of a drawing by
François Boucher.

Engraving of a drawing of *A Chinese
Couple in an Arbour* by François
Boucher.

Chinese Lovers.
*Model by P. Reinicke, c.1745. 5½
inches.*

Chinese Woman Dancing.
Model by P. Reinicke, c.1743. 6 inches.

Chinese Man with Bowl of Fruit.
Model by P. Reinicke, c.1743. 6 inches.

Chinese Man.
Model by P. Reinicke, c.1743. 5½ inches.

Chinese Man Holding a Conical Hat.
Model by P. Reinicke, c.1743. 5 inches.

Chinese Woman with a Fan.
Model by P. Reinicke, c.1743. 5 inches.

Inkstand with Chinese Figures.
Model by E. Meyer, c.1745. 14 inches wide.
This piece is in four separate parts consisting of the main tray, the centre group of a Chinese man with a European maidservant holding a sunshade, an inkwell in the form of a little Chinese boy whose shaven head comes off as a lid, and a sandbox in the form of a little Chinese girl whose head comes off as a lid. A similar inkstand was made later in 1762 for King Frederick the Great of Prussia.

Pair of Malabar Figures.
Models by F.E.Meyer, c.1750. 13 inches.

Pair of Seated Chinese Figures.
Models by J.F. Eberlein, c.1735. 6½ inches.
These figures were made as incense burners.

Two Figures of Chinese Boys with Nodding Heads.
Models by J.F. Eberlein and J.J. Kaendler, c.1750. 10 inches.
These figures have green cabbage leaves as hats; their heads
are suspended on metal spindles in order to make them nod
when touched.

Seated Chinese Figure.
Model by J.J. Kaendler, c.1737. 8 inches.
This figure was made as a table spice container for Count Brühl. This figure was made again in
a slightly different form by P. Reinicke in 1745 for the Prussian Court.

Chinese Man.
Model by P. Reinicke, c.1743. 6 inches.

Chinese Man with his Hands in his Sleeves.
Model by P. Reinicke, c.1743. 6 inches.

Blackamoor Girl.
Model by P. Reinicke, c.1748. 5 inches.
A blackamoor girl dressed in Turkish costume.

Blackamoor.
Model by P. Reinicke, c.1748. 5 inches.
A blackamoor in Turkish costume.

Blackamoor Servant.
Model by P. Reinicke, c.1748. 5 inches.
A servant boy holding a small footed tray with a sugar sifter.

Africa.
Model by P. Reinicke, c.1748. 5 inches.
This blackamoor figure is emblematic of Africa and
holds an elephant skin.

Female figure of Africa.
Model by P. Reinicke, c.1750. 5 inches.

OPPOSITE
Female Blackamoor with Covered Bowl.
Model by J.J. Kaendler, c.1748.
7½ inches.
This charming figure has a very attractive pierced basket.

America.
Model by P. Reinicke, c.1750. 5 inches.
This blackamoor figure, emblematic of America, wears a feathered cloak and head-dress, and has a parrot perched on her arm.

Satire

Satire and coarse and sometimes cruel humour were a part of life in the eighteenth century for both the nobility and the common people. They probably provided some relief from the rigid formality of the Court and the harshness of life, and this has continued into our own times with cartoons and media satirical programmes. But only the Meissen porcelain factory took it to such lengths in what has always been considered a decorative form. A careful look at these satirical groups will dispel the myth of the frivolous, sweet porcelain figure.

One of the most sardonic jokes must be Kaendler's *Tailor on a Goat*. This was made for the Chief Minister, Count Brühl who, as a renowned dandy, certainly counted his tailor as an important part of his entourage. However, the tailor's dreams of grandeur were looked on with a somewhat jaundiced eye by the Count when the tailor requested an invitation to dine at Court. But by placing the model of the tailor seated on a goat on the table as decoration, the Count felt he had allowed the tailor's social aspirations to go as far as they should. This model proved such a success that Kaendler made smaller models later on, with the addition of the tailor's wife and child as a pair. These were copied in great numbers by such factories as Derby.

Favourite subjects for Kaendler's wit were the court jesters Frohlic and Schmiedel. Court fools were a common feature at most courts for hundreds of years. This particular pair must have been great favourites, as they appear many times in different situations.

The other famous satirical figures are the Monkey Band, which have also been copied, both legitimately in admiration, and as outright fakes. These monkeys, known as the 'Affenkapelle' were probably inspired by sketches made by Christophe Hüet (designer of the rococo Cries of Paris) for the murals of monkeys dressed in human clothing that he painted at Chantilly.

Figures similar to those illustrated in this chapter may be found in the following museums:

Bayerischen Nationalmuseum, Munich, Germany.
British Museum, London, England.
Fenton House, London, England.
Victoria and Albert Museum, London, England.

The Gout Sufferer.
Model by J.J. Kaendler, c.1742.
7¹/₂ inches.
The look of pain on the man's face is wonderful. Are the bottles surrounding the pair full of medication or alcohol, which for many years was thought to cause gout?

The Earache Sufferer.
Model by J.J. Kaendler, c.1750.
7¹/₂ inches.
The old nurse appears to be holding a ring from which hang instruments presumably for probing the ears.

The Hypochondriac.
Model by J.J. Kaendler, c.1748. 8 inches.
This young man, who seems so sorry for himself, is being mocked by two Harlequins.

The Surprise.
Model by J.J. Kaendler, c.1748–50. 10 inches wide.
This group is taken from an engraving by Hogarth. The young woman holding a baby is accompanied by a lawyer holding a writ, and both have burst in upon a card game being held by the three at the table. The look of innocence on the face of the young man, and shock and horror on the part of the older man and woman, tell the tale in full.

The Cuckold.

Model by J.J. Kaendler, c.1741. 5 inches.

This group represents a satire on a court scandal. The records state: 'A group of Oberlandbaumeister Krösseln, two actors, one dressed as a woman who is putting feathers into the man's cap.'

BELOW LEFT

Schmiedel.

Model by J.J. Kaendler, c.1739. 21½ inches.

Life-like bust of 'Baron' Schmiedel, the postmaster, in white. The postmaster was known to have a fear of mice and a melancholic character, which seems to have been common amongst clowns.

BELOW RIGHT

Joseph Fröhlic.

Model by J.J. Kaendler, c.1738. 21 inches.

Life-like bust of court jester Joseph Fröhlic. In 1728 Fröhlic came from Salzkammergut, from the Bayruth Court to the Court of Augustus II in Dresden, where he remained until his death in 1763. Much beloved at Court, his figure was modelled many times. He was known to have a rough and wicked sense of humour. He also performed in town taverns with the little jester Christophe Kirshe, and was said to have ninety-nine jesters costumes provided by the King.

Tailor on a Goat.

Model by J.J. Kaendler, c.1741. 17 inches.

The King's chief administrator, Count Brühl, was a man famed for his clothes, and therefore his tailor was of paramount importance to him. However, when the tailor's ambitions made him ask for an invitation to dine at Court, the Count found this beyond the pale and had Kaendler make a figure of the tailor which he could place on his table and thus fulfil his empty promises.

Kaendler's undoubted sense of the ridiculous got the better of him and the model became a figure of fun.

OPPOSITE

Schindler.

Model by J.J. Kaendler, c.1735. 6½ inches.

Schindler was a court jester who worked along with Fröhlic and Schmiedel. The bagpipes are made from goatskin.

Court Jesters in a Sleigh.
Model by J.J. Kaendler, c.1737. 9 inches wide.
Schindler with Fröhlic dressed as a woman at one of the court festivities.

Drawing of a *Monkey Band Figure*, probably by Christophe Hüet.

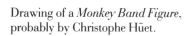

The Monkey Band.
Models by J.J. Kaendler, c.1749–55. 4 inches.
The monkey band was thought to have been made as a satire on the court orchestra. The exact date when these were made is not known, as the records for this period at the factory were destroyed. However, it is known that Madame de Pompadour ordered nineteen of these figures in 1753. Probably inspired by Hüet's murals at Chantilly.

Italian Comedy

Of all the thousands of models made by Kaendler in his years with Meissen, it is obvious that Harlequin and the other members of the Italian comedy (*commedia dell'arte*) were the ones that most caught his imagination. It was a theme that both he and his assistants were to return to time and time again over the years, and it is this series which really invokes the different fashions, from the wicked Harlequin jesters conveying the coarse wit of the times, through the charming rococo series made by Peter Reinicke for the Duke of Weissenfels, to Kaendler's attempt at the neo-classical revival in the late 1770s.

The origins of the Italian comedy, in particular Harlequin, are lost in the mists of time. However, actor-mimers portraying these characters were travelling all over Europe in the sixteenth century. Harlequin's costume, until the late seventeenth century, was a loose cover with patches and a ruff at the neck. In the eighteenth century, the costume was slimmed down and covered in lozenges of four colours: blue for love, red for anger, brown or mauve for constancy, and yellow for jealousy. The English pantomime and Punch and Judy shows originated from the Italian comedy.

In the seventeenth and eighteenth centuries these plays were impromptu affairs, and in many cases the actors were given very brief instructions only – in fact just the outline of the plot – sometimes written on a piece of paper and tacked to the side of the make-shift stage. It was left to the actors to call on their experience and natural talents to play out the memorized monologues, coarse jokes and acrobatic tricks.

The names of the main characters can sometimes be very confusing, as in many cases the same people seem to have different names, which does not always help to identify with accuracy the porcelain figures. For instance, women appeared late in the long history of *commedia dell'arte*, and did not wear masks all the time – as the men did in the beginning – but only a small velvet 'loup' to protect their beauty. They did not have clearly defined characters, but played *inamoratas*, servants, *ingénues*, mistresses, wantons, and matrons, as the occasion required. This probably explains why in Meissen they all seem to come under the same title 'Columbine'.

The characters mostly seen are Harlequin, Columbine, Pantalone, Scapin, Mezzetin, Scaramouche, the Captain, Dr Boloardo, Pulcinello, Tartaglio, Beltramc, Narcissino, and Pierrot.

The set of Italian comedy figures made by Peter Reinicke in 1743–44 were for Johann Adolph II, Duke of Weissenfels, probably as a present on his second marriage to a princess of the House of Coburg-Gotha shortly before his death at the age of 55.

The early Harlequin figures made by J.J. Kaendler were inspired by an

Augsberg book of engravings *c.*1700 sent to the factory by Count Brühl's friend Count Heinike.

In eighteenth-century France, the term 'Harlequin' was also used to describe a bucket of food consisting of small scraps of meat and vegetables. However, in modern times 'Harlequin' has entered the English language to describe a motley set of something, such as chairs, which are not exactly of the same design, but are similar enough not to offend the eye.

> 'Here's Harlequin as feather light,
> With Zany's tricks to you delight.'

Figures similar to those illustrated in this chapter may be found in the following museums:

Brooks Memorial Art Gallery, Memphis, Tennessee, USA.
British Museum, London, England.
Fitzwilliam Museum, Cambridge, England.
The Hermitage, Leningrad, USSR.
Museum of Art, Providence, Rhode Island, USA.
Museum für Kunst und Gewerbe, Hamburg, Germany.
Musée des Arts Décoratifs, Paris, France.
National Museum, Stockholm, Sweden.
Rijksmuseum, Amsterdam, Holland.
Smithsonian Institution, Washington, USA.
Victoria and Albert Museum, London, England.
Wadsworth Atheneum, Hartford, Connecticut, USA.
The Zwinger, Dresden, Germany.

Greeting Harlequin.
Model by J.J. Kaendler, c.1740. 6 inches.
The insincere look on Harlequin's face is so right for this figure. Riccoboni
wrote: 'The acting of the Harlequins before the seventeenth century was
nothing but a continual play of extravagant tricks, violent movements, and
outrageous rogueries. He was at once insolent, mocking, inept, clownish and
emphatically ribald.' This figure seems to encompass all of this. Probably
inspired by a painting by Watteau.

Scowling Harlequin.
Model by J.J. Kaendler, c.1738. 7½ inches.
Early figure of Harlequin with wonderful modelling. Note the absence of
even flowers on the base, which seems to add to the strength of the
modelling.

Harlequin Alarmed.
Model by J.J. Kaendler, c.1740. 7 inches.
The spots in the figure are where the glaze has missed and dirt
has penetrated the porcelain beneath. Playing card decoration
is a common feature on Harlequin figures, and although the
cards probably originated in the East, they appeared in Italy
in the fourteenth century, which is why they appear so
frequently on Italian comedy figures.

Seated Harlequin with a Drinking Glass.
Model by J.J. Kaendler, c.1740. 6½ inches.
The use of a goat-skin as the body of the bagpipes frequently
appears on Meissen figures.

Harlequin with a Bird.
Model by J.F. Eberlein, c.1745. 5½ inches.
This figure also exists with a cat seated on
the base, looking up at the bird.

Harlequin with a Jug.
Model by J.J. Kaendler, c.1740. 6½ inches.
This figure also exists with a date written on
the jug.

OPPOSITE
Seated Harlequin.
Model by J.J. Kaendler, c.1740. 4½ inches.
This seated Harlequin playing the bagpipes
appears frequently with small variations,
such as a different hat on his head or his
head turned at a different angle.

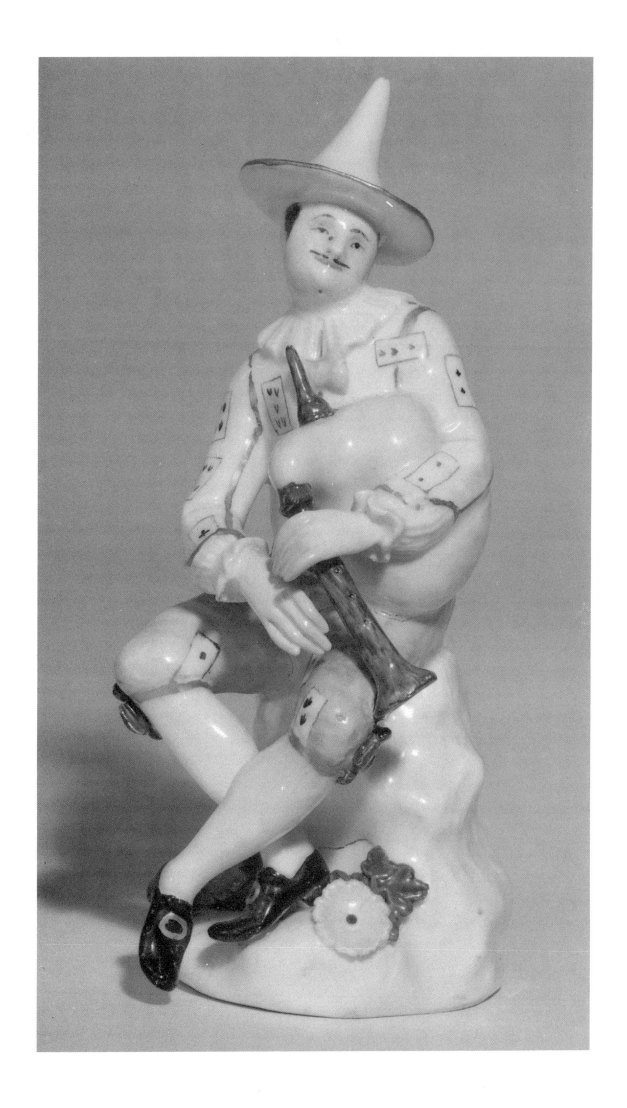

Harlequin Holding a Sausage.
Model by P. Reinicke, c.1744. 5½ inches.
The sausage appears frequently with Harlequin throughout
the centuries, and is still part of the English Punch and Judy
show.

Harlequin.
Model by P. Reinicke, c.1743. 5 inches.
This figure is known as part of the Duke of Weissenfels series
from an engraving by F. Joullain illustrating Riccoboni's book.
There is, however, also a seventeenth-century engraving of a
Harlequin by an unknown hand in exactly the same stance.

Harlequin.
Model by P. Reinicke, c.1744. 5 inches.
This figure is known as 'Harlequin Ancien' and is also part of
the Duke of Weissenfels series.

Peasant Figure dressed as Harlequin.
Model by J.J. Kaendler and J.F. Eberlein, c.1750. 4½ inches.
This figure is possibly that of the little jester Christophe Kirshe.

OPPOSITE
Harlequin Family.
Model by J.J. Kaendler, c.1740.
7 inches.
It is possible that the inspiration for
this group came from the
engravings of the Italian comedy
by G-J. Xavery.

Harlequin and Columbine.
Model by J.J. Kaendler, c.1750.
7 inches.
A romanticized version of this pair
in the rococo style.

Seated Harlequin and Columbine.
Models by J.J. Kaendler, c.1748. 4½ inches.
Columbine playing the hurdy gurdy and
Harlequin playing the bagpipes. The basic
shape of these figures appears several times in
various poses.

**Children dressed as Harlequin and
Columbine.**
Model by J.J. Kaendler, c.1755. 4½ inches.
This pair are from a set of figures of children
dressed in Italian comedy clothes, of which
these two are the most colourful.

OPPOSITE
Columbine.
Model by J.J. Kaendler, c.1765. 9 inches.
This figure comes from a small series made by
Kaendler at the end of the rococo period. A very
elegant figure, evocative of the period, it is also
very reminiscent of his shepherdesses.

Columbine.
Model by P. Reinicke, c.1744.
5 inches.
A figure from the Duke of Weissenfels
series, unusual in that she is holding
both her mask and castanets.

Dancing Columbine.
Model by P. Reinicke, c.1744.
5 inches.
A figure from the Duke of Weissenfels
series.

Columbine and Pantalone.
Model by J.J. Kaendler, c.1740. 6 inches.
Several versions of this group exist with different colouring and slightly different angles. The
group portrays Columbine as Pantalone's young wife making fun of her old husband.

Pantalone.
Model by J.J.Kaendler, c.1741. 6 inches.
This figure, known as 'Pantalone Ancien', was inspired by an engraving by J. Callot. Pantalone is believed originally to have been an eminent citizen of Venice. He is always depicted as an old man retired from business. Pantalone appears in various guises in the plays of Shakespeare, Molière and many others.

ABOVE
Pantalone.
Model by P. Reinicke, c.1744. 5 inches.
This figure is part of the series made for the Duke of Weissenfels.

Engraving of *Pantalone* by Jacques Callot.

Scaramouche Playing a Lute.
Model by J.J.Kaendler, c.1739–40. 6½ inches.
Scaramouche is said to have been remarkably strong, agile, and graceful, and sang to his own accompaniment on the lute.

Scaramouche.
Model by P. Reinicke, c.1744. 5 inches.
This figure comes from the series made for the Duke of Weissenfels.

Beltrame.
Model by P. Reinicke, c.1744. 5 inches.
This figure comes from the series made for the Duke of Weissenfels. Beltrame is said to have originated in Milan. His dress and appearance are very similar to that of Scapin.

TOP RIGHT
Engraving of *Beltrame* by F. Joullain.

Pulcinello.
Model by J.J. Kaendler, c.1748. 6 inches.
This figure appears in various different decorations and colours of mask. Although he is known in Roman mythology, his native town from the sixteenth century appears to have been Naples. He was said to have been 'self-centred, bestial, with no scruples, and because of the suffering from his physical deformity, was exceedingly cruel.'

Indifference.
Model by J.J. Kaendler, c.1742. 5½ inches.

Engraving of *Indifference* by François Boucher.

The Captain.
Model by P. Reinicke, c.1744. 5 inches.
This figure is from the series made for the Duke of
Weissenfels. The first Captain was Italian and
belonged to the fifteenth century. He was said to
have had eyes like steel and a bristling moustache,
and had an immense sword which quivered with
rage incessantly.

FAR RIGHT
Scapin.
Model by P. Reinicke, c.1744. 5 inches.
This figure is from the series made for the Duke of
Weissenfels. Scapin was a valet and general
handyman.

213

Mezzetin.
Model by P. Reinicke, c.1744.
5 inches.
This figure is from the series made for the Duke of Weissenfels. Mezzetin came into existence in the sixteenth century, when he was a double for Scapin, but he had gentler manners than Scapin.

FAR LEFT
Pedrolino.
Model by P. Reinicke, c.1744.
5 inches.
This figure is from the series made for the Duke of Weissenfels. Pedrolino dates from the second half of the sixteenth century. He appeared under various names such as Pierrot, Tartaglio, Pagliacci, and has also been portrayed by many artists such as Watteau.

Peirrot.
Model by P. Reinicke, c.1745. 5 inches.
The figure of Peirrot with his hands raised in surprise.

Child dressed as Beltrame.
Model by J.J. Kaendler, c.1750. 4½ inches.

Miniature figure of Harlequin.
Model by P. Reinicke, c.1750. 3 inches.
This figure of a Harlequin is a perfume bottle.

Appendices

Modellers

Johann Joachim Kaendler

Born in Arnsdorf near Dresden 15 June 1706. The son of the pastor of Fischbach, he was apprenticed to the famous Dresden court sculptor and owner of a carving workshop, Benjamin Thomae. Kaendler's forebears had also been stonecarvers. During the time that Thomae and his men worked on pieces for the palace. Augustus the Strong made frequent visits to watch the progress of the work, obviously noted Kaendler's skill, and on 22 June 1731 brought the young carver to work at Meissen. Kaendler worked at Meissen until his death on 18 May 1775.

Peter Reinicke

Born in Danzig in 1715. Reinicke joined Kaendler's workshop in 1743. Very early on he developed a talent for figure modelling. As well as helping Kaendler with his work he also personally made the series of Italian Comedy for the Duke of Weissenfels and many of the rococo series of Cries of Paris. He died on 2 May 1768.

Friedrich Elias Meyer

Born in Erfurt in 1724. Meyer started work in Kaendler's workshop on 10 May 1748 as a sculptor and modeller. He was highly regarded from the very beginning, but there is very little record of his work in the Meissen archives. Although mention is made frequently about the small heads on his figures, this was more in keeping with his very strong French rococo style. This style was greatly admired by King Frederick II of Prussia, and consequently he went to work in King Frederick's factory in Berlin in 1761.

Johann Friedrich Eberlein

Born in Dresden in 1696 Eberlein started work as a sculptor for the French metal founder Vinache. He went to work at Meissen for Kaendler in 1734. Although older and more experienced than Kaendler, he was content to work under the Model Master. His own independent work can sometimes be picked out by the almost Oriental slant to the eyes of the figures. He died 20 July 1749.

Johann Gottlieb Ehder

Born in Leipzig in 1717. Ehder was the son of a stonemason. He did a lot of fine finishing work to Kaendler's figures apart from his own individual work, such as extremely delicate pierced work on a watch case. He died after an accident in 1750.

Artists

François Boucher (1703–1776)
Jean Baptiste Le Prince (1734–1781)
Edmé Bouchardon (1693–1762)
Marcellus Laroon (1653–1702)
Jean-Antoine Watteau (1684–1721)
Jacques Callot (1592–1635)
Christophe Hüet (Died 1759)
Jacques le Hay (Died early eighteenth century)
Luigi Riccoboni (1675–1753)
Christoph Weigel (Died 1725)
Pierce Tempest (1650–1717)
William Hogarth (1650–1717)

Museums

England	Bedford	The Cecil Higgins Museum
	Cambridge	The Fitzwilliam Museum
	London	The British Museum
		Fenton House
		The Victoria and Albert Museum
		Waddesden Manor
	Oxford	The Ashmoleon Museum
Germany	Ansbach	The Residenz
	Berlin	Kunstgewerbemuseum
	Cologne	Kunstgewerbemuseum
	Frankfurt	Museum für Kunsthandwerk
	Hamburg	Museum für Kunst und Gewerber
	Mannheim	Reiss-museum
	Munich	Bayerischen Nationalmuseum
	Dresden	The Zwinger
France	Paris	Musée du Louvre
		Musée des Arts Décoratifs
	Sèvres	Musée Nationale de Ceramique
	Dijon	Musée de Dijon
Holland	Amsterdam	Rijksmuseum
Italy	Naples	Villa Floridiana
		Capo di Monte Castle
	Rome	Museo Capitolino
Sweden	Stockholm	National Museum
Switzerland	Bern	Bernishes Historisches Museum
	Zurich	Kunsthaus
USA	Baltimore	Museum of Art
	Connecticut	The Wadsworth Atheneum, Hartford
	Florida	Cummer Gallery of Art, Jacksonville
	Georgia	The High Museum, Atlanta
	New York	The Metropolitan Museum
	Rhode Island	Museum of Art, Providence
	Tennessee	Brooks Memorial Art Gallery, Memphis
	Washington	The Smithsonian Institution
USSR	Leningrad	The Hermitage

Chronology of the Meissen Porcelain Factory 1700–75

1700   Kaolin is discovered and mined near Schneeberg.

1701   Böttger flees from Berlin to Wittenberg; is seized by Augustus II and sent to Dresden.

1702   Böttger and Tschirnhaus meet for the first time.

1705   The first experiments to make porcelain are started when Böttger moved to Albrechtsburg.

1706   Böttger was put into 'protective custody' in the Fortress of Königstein.

1707   New laboratory was installed at Jungfernbastei for high temperature firing. First brownish-red stoneware similar to that made by the Chinese was produced.

1708   On 15 January the first small white porcelain bowl was produced.
On 11 October Ehrenfried W. von Tschirnhaus died.

1709   Böttger announces on 29 March the invention of hard paste porcelain.

1710   January announcements were made in four languages of the invention of hard paste porcelain.

1711   First mention of the modeller Georg Fritzsche.

1712   Twenty-three craftsmen were employed, plus apprentices being trained by J.J. Irminger, silversmith to the Dresden Court.

1713   The Leipzig Easter Fair produced the first sale of white hard paste porcelain.

1714   A showroom was opened in Dresden.

1717   On 28 August the King was presented with the first example of blue underglaze painting.

1719   The first leakage of the secret of making hard paste porcelain came about with the defection of Stöltziel to Vienna.
13 March – Böttger dies of alcoholism and loneliness.
Augustus II gives the first order for porcelain for his New Japanese Palace.

1720   Stöltziel, disillusioned with Vienna, returns to Meissen, bringing with him Johann Gregorius Höroldt, who was to become Meissen's most famous painter.

1721   Craftsmen unhappy about the delay in the payment of their wages, sometimes as long as two months.

1722   First coloured decoration porcelain sent for sale at the Leipzig Fair.

1723   Introduction of quality control.

1724   Höroldt officially receives the title of Court Painter.

1725   The factory now employs forty-one people including salesmen, painters and apprentices under Höroldt.

1727   Johann Gottlieb Kirchner, the modeller, joins the factory, together with J.C.L.Lücke. Large orders for porcelain received from Paris.

1728   Kirchner dismissed.

1729   Lucke dismissed.

1730   Kirchner re-employed as a master sculptor.

1731   Augustus II takes over the directorship of the factory.
Höroldt made Artistic Director of the factory.
Johann Joachim Kaendler employed as a modeller.

1733   Augustus II died in February. Succeeded by his son Augustus III, elector of Saxony and King of Poland.
J.J. Kaendler made Model Master.

1734   Athanas Manasses demands exclusive rights for all trade with Turkey.

1735   Johann Frederick Eberlein employed as assistant modeller to Kaendler.
Count Heinrich von Brühl, Prime Minister of Saxony, becomes the Director General of the factory, with permission to order unlimited amounts of porcelain for himself.

1736   The painter Lowenfinck defects to Bayreuth.
Kaendler produces the Carillion for the Organ in the Palace Chapel.

1739   Johann Gottlieb Ehder employed to work with Kaendler.

1740   The factory had 218 employees.

1741   Augustus III sends a large amount of French engravings to the factory.

1743   Peter Reinicke employed as a modeller.

1748   Frederick Elias Meyer engaged as a modeller.

1749   J.J. Kaendler's cousin Christian Heinrich Kaendler put in charge of all the moulds.

1750   J.J. Kaendler went to Paris to deliver a large porcelain mirror as a wedding present from Augustus III to his daughter on her marriage to the Dauphin of France.

1751   571 employees.

1756   Seven Years' War starts. A large amount of the employees either fled or were sent to safety. J.J. Kaendler stayed.

1757   Frederick of Prussia took possession of the factory and leased it to his military procuror, Schimmelmann.

1762   Kaendler refuses to go to Berlin and manages to evade any confrontations between himself and Frederick on Frederick's numerous visits to the factory.

1763   August III and Count Brühl both died.

1775   January, J.C. Höroldt died.
May, J.J. Kaendler died.

Bibliography

Bacci, Mina, *European Porcelain*.

Beall, Karen F., *Cries and Itinerate Trades*, (Dr Ernst Hanswedell, Hamburg).

Benezit, *Dictionary of Painters, Sculptors and Engravers*. Library Gründe, 1961.

Berling, Dr K., *Festival Publication to Commemorate the 200th Jubilee of the Oldest European China Factory, Meissen* (The Royal Saxon China Manufactury, Meissen, 1910).

Catnach, J., *The Cries of London*.

Ducharte, Pierre Louis, *The Italian Comedy* (Harrap, 1929).

Honey, Wm. B., *German Porcelain* (Faber and Faber, 1954).

Jean-Richard, Pierette, *L'Oeuvre Gravé de François Boucher* (Editions des Musées Nationaux, 1978).

Larousse, *Gastronomy* (Hamlyn, 1961).

Larousse, *Encyclopedia of Mythology* (Hamlyn, 1959).

Le Hay, Jacques, *Receuil de Cent Estampes Representant Differantes Nations du Levant*.

Lumsden, J., *The Cries of London*.

Massin, *Les Cries de la Ville* (Gallimard, 1978).

Mazour, G., *Russia Past and Present* (Macmillan, 1951).

Morley-Fletcher, Hugo, *Meissen Porcelain in Colour* (Barrie and Jenkins, 1971).

Newman, Michael, *Die deutschen Porzellan – Manufakturen* (Klinkhardt and Bierman, Braunschweig, 1977).

Opie, I and P., *The Oxford Dictionary of Nursery Rhymes* (OUP, 1951).

Pauls-Eisenbeiss, Dr Erika, *German Porcelain in the Eighteenth Century* (Barrie and Jenkins, 1972).

Palacios, Alvan Gonzales, *The Age of Louis XV* (Hamlyn, 1966).

Riccoboni, Luigi, *Histoire du Théatre Italien*, published in Paris in the eighteenth century.

Röntgen, Robert E., *The Book of Meissen* (Schiffer, 1984).

Rückert, Rainer, *Meissener Porzellan 1710–1810* (Hirmer, 1966).

Sand, Maurice, *Masques et Bouffons* (Michel Lévy, Paris, 1860).

Schröder, Thomas, *Jacques Callot* (Verlagsgellshaft, undated).

Shadwell, Thomas, *London*, published in eighteenth century.

Smith, John Thomas, *The Cries of London*, published in nineteenth century.

Strauss, Ralph, *Eighteenth Century London Diversions*, published in nineteenth century.

Tempest, Pierce, *The Cryes of the City of London Drawne after the Life by M. Lauron* (Printed and Sold by Henry Overton at the White Horse without Newgate London, 1733).

Tuer, Andrew, *Old London Street Cries* (Field and Tuer, 1885).

Walcha, Otto, *Meissener Porzellan* (Verlug der Kunst, Dresden, 1973).

Weigel, Christoph, *Miners*, published in early eighteenth century.

Wyss, Robert L., *Porcelain Collection Kocher* (Editions Stämpfli & Cie, Bern, 1965).

Index

INDEX